T5-ARZ-353

Touche Ross International

THE TOUCHE ROSS GUIDE TO INTERNATIONAL INSOLVENCY

◆ ◆

Covering Australia, Canada, United Kingdom and United States

Probus Publishing Company
Chicago, Illinois

332.75
T72t

© 1989, Touche Ross International

ALL RIGHTS RESERVED. No part of this publication may be reproduced, stored in a retrieval system, or transmitted in any form or by any means, electronic, mechanical, photocopying, recording or otherwise, without the prior written permission of the publisher and the copyright holder.

This publication is designed to provide accurate and authoritative information in regard to the subject matter covered. It is sold with the understanding that the publisher is not engaged in rendering legal, accounting or other professional service.

FROM A DECLARATION OF PRINCIPLES JOINTLY ADOPTED BY A COMMITTEE OF THE AMERICAN BAR ASSOCIATION AND A COMMITTEE OF PUBLISHERS.

Library of Congress Cataloging in Publication Data Available

ISBN: 1-55738-036-8

MB

Printed in the United States of America

1   2   3   4   5   6   7   8   9   0

PREFACE

Dealing with the problems of companies in foreign jurisdictions is seldom safe without the benefit of professional assistance from local experts in the countries concerned. However, it is clearly of much value to have a broad understanding of the law and procedures involved in order more quickly to grasp the strategies recommended.

This book, written by Touche Ross partners and staff specializing in insolvency and corporate recovery advice together with eminent lawyers also specializing in these matters, is designed to provide such an understanding.

In many cases it is easier to write a book about legal procedures than about those extra-legal procedures commonly operated. When preparing this book we had to bear in mind that practices often vary, and that it would be difficult to get the unanimous agreement of accountants and lawyers as to the way insolvency law in any one country works in practice. It is often only the personal judgement of the insolvency accountant or lawyer which tells him how a particular matter should be handled. Practices and standards differ enormously from country to country and from practitioner to practitioner, and indeed what is the right procedure for the failure of a major multinational company may be quite inappropriate in the case of a small sole trader. It is often left to the practitioner to interpret and use the available law as best he can.

Partners and staff of Touche Ross International offices, as members of one of the world's leading public accounting organizations, have amassed considerable experience in advising banks on their problem loans and in assisting distressed companies in the formulation and execution of corporate recovery plans at both national and international levels.

We hope that this book, written as a result of the experience we have gained, will provide practical assistance to readers who face problems involving insolvency or corporate recovery situations in the four major countries described.

iii

University Libraries
Carnegie Mellon University
Pittsburgh, Pennsylvania 15213

ACCREDITATION

The Guide has been compiled under the control of an Editorial Committee of the following partners in Touche Ross International member firms:

Tony Houghton — Executive Editor, UK
Ian Struthers — Australia
Michael W. Mackey — Canada
Jim Illson — USA

We gratefully acknowledge the contributions of Messrs Stuart E. Hertzberg and Dennis S. Kayes of the law firm Pepper, Hamilton & Scheetz in respect of the USA chapter, and of Mr George Cihra of the law firm of Borden & Elliott in respect of the Canadian chapter.

We are also grateful for the time and assistance given by our colleagues within Touche Ross in the preparation of this publication. In particular we wish to thank:

Australia	Glenn Crisp
	Andrew Campbell
	David Anderson
	Jim Downey
Canada	James A. Morrison
	Robert D. Merkley
United Kingdom:	Malcolm Fillmore

A. R. Houghton

AUSTRALIA

Australia
Table of Contents

Contents

AUSTRALIA

NOTE ON LEGAL SYSTEMS AND PROCEDURES IN AUSTRALIA

Australia has followed the English pattern of separate legislation for corporations and individuals.

Colonial bankruptcy and insolvency jurisdictions were established in the Australian States during the 19th century. At the turn of the century the Commonwealth Constitution gave Federal Parliament power to legislate with respect to bankruptcy and insolvency. The first Commonwealth Bankruptcy Act was enacted in 1924 and commenced in 1928. It was an amalgamation of British and colonial legislation. In 1966 the Bankruptcy Act of 1924 was repealed and replaced by a new Bankruptcy Act, which commenced operation in 1968. The 1966 Act introduced a new consolidated procedure for private arrangements avoiding bankruptcy and deviated from many of the English and Australian precedents. The Bankruptcy Act of 1966 is still in operation today subject to certain amendments made since its enactment.

Company law has always been administered by the individual States and Territories. Legislation of the Australian States and Territories generally followed English legislation from the mid-19th century; however, there was a lack of conformity between the States.

The Uniform Companies Acts of 1961-62, passed by all the Australian States as separate but closely parallel State Acts, represented a comprehensive attempt to standardize legislation between the States. With few exceptions, it was based on the Great Britain Companies Act of 1948.

Since then, the Federal and State Governments executed a formal agreement of cooperation to provide uniform company laws. Consequently, a substantially uniform Companies Code has operated in all states and the Australian Capital Territory (A.C.T.) since July 1, 1982 and in the Northern Territory since July 1, 1986. Where procedures between the states differ, this is noted in the text.

INSOLVENCY PRACTITIONERS

Most Insolvency Practitioners are accountants in public practice, usually belonging to one of the professional bodies, such as the Institute of Chartered Accountants in Australia or the Australian Society of Accountants. Both the Institute and the

Society maintain subcommittees in the field of insolvency, representing both corporate and noncorporate insolvency.

The majority of registered trustees and registered and official Liquidators are members of the Insolvency Practitioners Association of Australia, which is an organization that fosters the professional competence of insolvency practitioners.

INDIVIDUAL INSOLVENCY

To accept an appointment under the Bankruptcy Act an insolvency practitioner must be a registered trustee. To qualify as a registered trustee a natural person (usually a public accountant) must apply to the court and provide full details of professional qualifications and experience. The Official Receiver then interviews the applicant, makes enquiries and files a report with the court. If accepted, the trustee is registered, a bond is required from him, and a certificate of registration is issued to him.

The Official Trustee (a government body) is also qualified to act as a trustee. If no consent to act in an administration is forthcoming from a registered trustee, then the Official Trustee will act as Trustee of the Estate.

A trustee in bankruptcy (a registered trustee or the Official Trustee) may be the trustee of a Bankrupt Estate, or a Part X Administration; he may also be an interim trustee or a controlling trustee. An interim trustee is the title given to the Official Trustee or a registered trustee appointed by the court to take control of a debtor's property after the presentation of a creditor's petition but before sequestration. A controlling trustee is a registered trustee, or occasionally the Official Trustee, who acts to 'control' the affairs of a debtor prior to the holding of a meeting of creditors to consider a proposed arrangement under Part X of the Bankruptcy Act.

Some further textual terms concerning administrators or administrative bodies in respect to individual insolvency include the following:

Official Receivers. These are public officials under the control of the court who employ officers to assist them. There are Official Receivers for each bankruptcy district in Australia and each is appointed by the Governor General. The Official Receivers jointly constitute the body corporate known as the Official Trustee Bankruptcy.

The Registrar in Bankruptcy. For each bankruptcy district there is a Registrar in Bankruptcy and Deputy Registrars. The Registrars are officials independent of the Court appointed under the Bankruptcy Act to be custodians of Court documents and to supervise administrative work under the Bankruptcy Act. The Registrars are required to aid and be auxiliary to Official Receivers, Officers, and other persons having functions under the Bankruptcy Act.

The Bankruptcy Court. This refers to any Court having jurisdiction in bankruptcy under the Act and includes the Federal Court of Australia, and the Supreme Courts of all States of Australia.

The Inspector-General in Bankruptcy. This is the permanent public service department head in charge of bankruptcy who is responsible to the Federal Attorney-General (the Minister). The duties of this department include:

- Making such enquiries and investigations as the minister directs;
- Making enquiries and conducting investigations with respect to the conduct of trustees and administrations under the Bankruptcy Act;
- Administering and obtaining periodic reports from Registrars, Official Receivers, registered trustees, and other officers responsible for carrying out the Act.

CORPORATE INSOLVENCY

Administrators appointed over the affairs of a company pursuant to the Companies Code are required to have certain attributes and qualifications before they are eligible to hold such positions. The following is a summary of the different forms of administrator appointed under the Companies Code and the requirements qualifying them to hold such offices:

(i) **Registered Liquidators.** Only registered liquidators may act as liquidators of companies. The only exception is in the case of a members' voluntary winding up of a proprietary company that is an exempt proprietary company or that is a subsidiary of a public company. Only a registered liquidator may be appointed to a company as a receiver or receiver/manager or a scheme manager or scheme trustee. To become a registered liquidator, a person must apply to the commission providing full details of professional qualifications and of experience in public accounting practice and in the administration of liquidated or bankrupt estates. If accepted, a liquidator is registered and a security is required from him.

(ii) **Official Liquidators.** An official liquidator is one who is qualified to act as a liquidator in Court windings-up under the National Companies Code. Only official liquidators may be appointed in a court winding up or as provisional liquidators by the court. Official liquidators are registered liquidators who have been additionally approved and registered as official liquidators by the Corporate Affairs Commission.

(iii) **Provisional Liquidators.** These are official liquidators who have been appointed provisionally by the Court on or after the filing of a winding-up application, and before a winding-up order is made or, where there·is an appeal against that order, before a decision in the appeal is made.

(iv) **Official Managers.**   These are appointed when creditors resolve to place a company under official management pursuant to Part XI of the Companies Code.   They need not be a registered liquidator as is the case with other insolvency administrations, although the person appointed will often be a registered liquidator.   An official manager can be any person who is not the auditor of the Company, is not an officer of a corporation that is a mortgagee of property of the company, and who is not insolvent or under administration.

(v) **Scheme Managers or Trustees.**   Scheme Managers or Scheme Trustees appointed under Part VIII of the Companies Code to administer arrangements and reconstructions by a company must be registered liquidators and have the requisite independence as prescribed by the Companies Code.

(vi) **Receivers or Receivers/Managers.**   Administrators appointed as Receivers or Receivers and Managers of a Company are also required to be registered liquidators.   They must also possess the independence prescribed by the Code.

In addition to the requirements under the Companies Code, and Bankruptcy Act governing the independence and other requirements of liquidators, trustees and other Insolvency Administrators, the professional bodies such as the Institute of Chartered Accountants in Australia, the Australian Society of Accountants and the Insolvency Practitioners Association of Australia, have issued Ethical Rulings and Insolvency Standards that Insolvency Practitioners are required to adhere to.   One such requirement is that an insolvency practitioner may not accept an appointment in respect to an insolvent client if any person in the practice has, or during the previous two years has had, a continuing professional relationship with the client.

1. TYPES OF BUSINESS ENTITY

The principal types of business entity in Australia are limited companies, partnerships, and sole traders.

1.1 Limited Companies

The most common business entity is the limited company, which is controlled by the provisions of the Companies Code in each State. It is a legal entity distinct from its shareholders, whose liability is limited to the nominal value of their shareholdings in the company. A company can own property and can sue and be sued in its own name. Basic information concerning every limited company must be filed for public reference at the office of the Corporate Affairs Commission in each State.

Limited companies may be either 'public' or 'private.' A private company must have the word "Proprietary" or the abbreviation "Pty." in its name. The financial statements of every public company must be independently audited, although at present only public companies have to file their statements with the Corporate Affairs Commission.

No minimum capital is prescribed for either public or private companies. Every company is managed by a board of directors; employees have no legal right to representation on such boards.

The distinguishing features of private companies include the following:

a. the minimum number of shareholders is two and the maximum fifty (excluding employees and ex-employees), whereas the minimum number for a public company is five;

b. the transfer of shares is subject to restrictions;

c. it cannot invite the public to subscribe for its shares or debentures; and

d. it does not have to publish its financial statements.

A ready-formed private company can be purchased without delay from accountants or solicitors. If it is then desired to adopt a particular name for the company (and the desired name is available), a fee is payable to effect the change.

1.2 Partnerships

A partnership (sometimes referred to as a 'firm') is not a legal entity distinct from its individual partners. Each partner is jointly (and in New South Wales, severally) liable for all contractual debts and obligations incurred by the partnership; the liability of partners for torts and other wrongs is joint and several in all States and Territories.

A partnership must comprise at least two partners and not more than twenty. (Some professional partnerships are exempt from this requirement.)

Although a partnership is normally established by written agreement between the partners, there is no legal requirement for such an agreement.

A partnership does not have to publish or file its financial statements.

If a business carries on its trade under a name that does not consist of the names of all its proprietors, its trading name must be registered under the Business Names Act in each State. By their nature, most partnerships are subject to this requirement. Registration is simple and inexpensive.

Partnerships are usually either:

a. lawyers, accountants, and the like, whose professional rules do not allow them to practice with limited liability; or

b. small concerns that have not sought the protection of limited liability.

Limited partnerships are rarely met because of the ease with which private limited companies can be formed.

1.3 Sole Traders

Any individual owning and operating a business alone is generally referred to as a 'sole trader.' If a trading name other than that of the proprietor is used, it must be registered under the Business Names Act. Otherwise there are no statutory requirements regarding the registration of a sole trader.

1.4 Other Business Entities

Other trading entities include the following:

a.   joint ventures;

b.   cooperative societies;

c.   friendly and provident societies; and

d.   unlimited companies.

These organizations are rarely involved in insolvency proceedings and are therefore not referred to further in this Guide.

2. REORGANIZATION PROCEDURES

The procedures to be followed in the reorganization of limited Companies differ from those applicable to partnerships, joint debtors, and individuals. Accordingly, the reorganization procedures in this chapter have been divided between those applicable to limited Companies and those applicable to partnerships, joint debtors, and private individuals.

A. Limited Companies

The principal reorganization procedures applicable to limited Companies are:

*   Schemes of Arrangement
*   Official Management
*   Receivership

Receivership is a procedure allowing a secured creditor to enforce its floating charge security. It is not strictly a reorganization procedure; however, it usually permits an insolvent business to continue operations. Members' Voluntary Liquidation is included as a Terminal Procedure in Chapter 3; however, it is often used as a means of reorganising a Company group.

2.1 Schemes of Arrangement — A Scheme of Arrangement is a statute-approved procedure permitting a Company to make a compromise or arrangement binding on all its creditors/members (either or both), or classes of either or both. The scheme must provide an expected benefit to the parties concerned. There is a modification or adjustment of the normal rights and obligations of creditors or members (either or both) vis-a-vis the Company. The Companies Code provides the machinery for effecting such modification or adjustment, so as to make the arrangement binding on all persons if assented to by a substantial majority of those persons concerned.

A scheme is a flexible form of administration as it can vary from situations that provide for a compromise of creditors' debts whereby creditors agree to accept less than 100 cents on the dollar in full satisfaction of their debts, to other situations involving a moratorium on the payment of debts for a certain period, while the Company returns to financial health as a result of a rationalization or reorganization of its business operations.

Creditors potentially can receive a greater financial return than they could from liquidation, and there is the further advantage of deriving profits through continued trading with the Company during the term of the scheme and thereafter.

However, a scheme cannot be implemented immediately, as it requires the sanction of a meeting of creditors. If it is a formal scheme, it also requires the sanction of the Supreme Court and the Corporate Affairs Commission. A scheme is appropriate when an insolvent Company has good prospects of trading profitably so that future creditors are not at risk of remaining unpaid.

As the procedures for approving a scheme will usually take eight to ten weeks, such administrations are most appropriate when early identification of insolvency is achieved. They are also expensive in terms of legal fees and the substantial amount of work required by the proposed administrator.

Other advantages in the implementation of a scheme in preference to entering into liquidation are that a scheme will avoid restrictions on the carrying on of business and possible rescission of contracts in progress that could follow the commencement of liquidation, and, secondly, a scheme may allow the realisation of accumulated tax losses by either existing shareholders or third parties.

However, schemes of arrangement do have major disadvantages including:

(i)   They require the support of a large majority of creditors, and it is difficult to persuade a sufficient proportion of the creditors that their position will be improved by allowing the Company to continue trading.

(ii) They are cumbersome to operate and difficult for creditors to monitor.

(iii) They normally only operate when the Company has a considerable asset base.

Because of the above difficulties, schemes of arrangement are used infrequently.

A scheme of arrangement should only be proposed and effected if.it has commercial viability; otherwise it will be rejected by creditors or members.

2.1.1 Types of Scheme — The types of arrangements or compromises that a Company may negotiate with its creditors/members are wide-ranging. They may be as simple as a moratorium arrangement with creditors or as complex as a scheme involving reconstruction and amalgamation of companies or company groups, with consequent reorganization of share and loan capital modifying the rights of ordinary unsecured creditors, secured debenture holders, and various types of shareholders.

Formal Schemes of Arrangement — The machinery for securing approval of a scheme and for other administrative requirements in connection with the administration of a scheme are contained in Part VIII of the national companies and securities legislation (the Companies Code) and in various State Supreme Court Rules governing Court procedures.

Part VIII of the Code refers to "Arrangements and Reconstructions." The Forms of Scheme referred to in Part VIII of the Companies Code are as follows:

- A compromise or arrangement - proposed between a Company and its creditors/members (Section 315(1)).
- A reconstruction of a corporation or an amalgamation of corporations (Section 317).
- The acquisition of shares from shareholders under a 'Scheme of Contract' (Section 318).

The Companies Code does not set guidelines for a scheme of arrangement, it merely provides the machinery for a scheme to be agreed to, to be given the discretionary sanction of the Court, and as a result to be made binding on nonconsenting minorities. What the scheme does and provides for must be contained in the written scheme document.

A formal scheme of arrangement occurs only if the Court exercises its discretion to approve a proposed scheme (Section 315(4)(b)). The Court may grant its approval subject to such alterations or conditions as it thinks just (Section 315(6)).

Alternative (Informal) Schemes of Arrangement — A Company may make an informal arrangement with its creditors or an arrangement pursuant to Section 412 of the Companies Code as an alternative to a formal scheme of arrangement under Part VIII of the Companies Code.

An arrangement under Section 412 is relevant only to a situation in which a Company will be voluntarily wound up, and is likely to be used only as an alternative to the Liquidator's power to make individual compromises under Section 377(1)(c) of the Companies Code. Section 412 arrangements provide a mechanism for a Company's liquidator and the Company's creditors to make an arrangement that becomes binding on all creditors by reason of the agreement of a special majority of them.

As there is no legislative backing for the scheme to bind nonconsenting creditors, it is critical that all creditors agree to the scheme because a single dissenting creditor or an unknown creditor can upset the scheme by proceeding with their rights to take legal recovery action or petition the Court to have the company placed in liquidation. Therefore, for such a scheme to be effective, it is necessary to obtain individual written agreements from all creditors evidencing the arrangements under the scheme.

Usually, informal schemes are only appropriate when a Company has a relatively small number of creditors and good relations exist between them and the Company.

The major advantage for a Company to have an informal scheme in comparison to a formal scheme is that it can be implemented far more quickly and is less expensive in terms of professional fees. A further advantage of informal schemes is that they often allow a more flexible and commercial approach to be taken in reconstruction or reorganization of the Company's affairs.

2.1.2 Procedure — If a Company wishes to enter into a scheme of arrangement with its creditors or members, it must:

- Compile the necessary information for the formal proposal of a scheme, securing initial consensus from major creditors as to the possibility of success, and have solicitors draft the scheme document.

- Apply to the Court for an order permitting a scheme meeting (if a formal scheme) to be convened, simultaneously providing the Corporate Affairs Commission with information about the scheme.

- Hold a scheme meeting and secure the required special resolutions of creditors/members or classes thereof; and

- Secure an order of the Court approving the scheme (if a formal scheme).

2.2 Official Management — Official Management is an arrangement pursuant to Part XI of the Companies Code between a Company and its creditors, involving a temporary statutory moratorium by unsecured creditors (preventing legal proceedings being taken), during which period the Company trades under the control of an official manager, with the object of repaying creditors in full. Legal remedies normally available to unsecured creditors, but which are restricted by Official Management, include the ordinary remedies of proceeding to judgment and levying execution on a judgment and making application to the Court to wind up the Company. The intention is to enforce a moratorium and to replace individual repayments with the orderly application of Company assets. The rights of secured creditors remain unaffected by Official Management. An official management administration is only appropriate to a Company that is unable to pay its debts but that has reasonable prospects of rehabilitation. There must be a strong possibility that as a result of the Company continuing to carry on business, it will be able to pay is creditors 100 cents on the dollar during the moratorium period. If the objective of paying creditors in full becomes unattainable, the administration must be terminated by the Official Manager and he must take steps to place the Company into liquidation.

One of the major advantages of official management is that it can be implemented reasonably quickly, after a review of the Company's affairs by an insolvency specialist has established that the Company has strong prospects of paying all creditors in full through continued trading.

The prospects of a Company being rescued through official management are largely dependent upon the early recognition by the directors and/or external advisers of the Company's insolvency before it becomes too insolvent where resuscitation will normally require a substantial restructuring or rationalization of the Company's affairs. It is not designed to cater for such situations as it is generally too restrictive in terms of the official manager being unable to readily sell substantial assets outside the ordinary course of business or refinance the Company's borrowings in an effort to reduce gearing, increase profitability, and improve cash flow.

Practically, official management is not commonly used to rescue a Company from financial failure because management does not traditionally seek specialist advice early enough in the Company's downward cycle to enable it to be implemented.

2.2.1 Procedure for Appointment of Official Manager — Official Management may be initiated voluntarily by a Directors' Meeting, which determines that the Company is unable to pay its debts and resolves to convene a meeting of creditors for the purpose of placing the Company under official management for a specified period and appointing a particular person, usually a registered liquidator, as official manager. Official management may also be initiated by a creditor with an unsatisfied judgment of at least $1,000 who requests the Company to convene a meeting of creditors for the same purpose. Accordingly, official management is a nonjudicial procedure that may be initiated without an application to the Court.

The official management commences when and if creditors at the duly convened meeting pass the required special resolution. Upon the appointment of an official manager, the directors cease to hold office and the official manager becomes responsible for the management of the Company and he assumes all the duties and powers of the Directors.

The period of official management and hence the length of the moratorium is determined by the creditors who may specify a period not exceeding three years. However, extensions for further periods of twelve months can be made.

2.2.2 Duties and Powers of Official Manager — Official management envisages that a Company can be rehabilitated to a position of solvency through careful and efficient management of its business activities, and not as a result of a major rationalization or reconstruction of its affairs, involving the disposal of substantial assets outside the usual course of its normal business activities. There are restrictions pursuant to Section 349 of the Companies Code on an official manager disposing of assets other than in the ordinary course of the Company's business. He is under no restrictions when the value of the asset to be disposed of, together with the prices received for assets already sold outside the ordinary course of business, does not exceed $5,000. However, when the aggregate value of assets to be sold and previously sold is between $5,000 and $20,000, he requires either the consent of the Committee of Management, the leave of the Court or the consent of creditors given by special resolution. When the aggregate value of assets exceeds $20,000, he requires the leave of the Court or consent of creditors given by special resolution. A further restriction imposed on the ability of an official manager to restructure the Company's affairs is that he can only mortgage or charge any property of the Company with the consent of creditors given by special resolution or leave of the Court.

During the period of official management, an official manager may:

- Apply moneys that became available to him among the Company's common creditors, after allowing for the costs, expenses, and liabilities of official management.

- Conduct an examination of the circumstances giving rise to the Company's insolvency.

- Take steps to voluntarily wind up the affairs of the Company if he forms the opinion that continuance of the official management will not enable the Company to pay its debts.

In essence, the official manager is responsible for managing the Company back to solvency while the Company retains its basic characteristics and its fundamental business undertakings.

2.2.3 Termination of Official Management

2.2.3 Termination of Official Management — An official management is brought to an end either because:

- The statutory time period has expired;
- It has fulfilled its function of restoring the Company to solvency; or
- It has failed to fulfil its purposes and should be brought to an end, often leading to the liquidation of the Company.

The official manager may permit the period of the official management to expire, whether the Company has been successful in its official management or not. More satisfactorily, he may take specific action to bring the official management to an end by:

- Seeking an order of the Court; or
- Convening a meeting of members and creditors to arrange for a creditors' voluntary winding up.

Creditors themselves may require the official manager to bring the official management to an end. They may force this by passing a special resolution at any meeting of creditors of which special notice has been given. They may also apply directly to the Court for an order of termination.

2.3 Receivership — A Receivership is an administrative procedure by which a Receiver, or Receiver and Manager, is appointed to administer property. This administration may be limited to mere protection of one particular item of property or it may extend to general control overall of the property, and affairs of a corporation, including power to realize property.

Usually receivership does not involve a reorganization of Company affairs, except to a small extent with trading on, and cannot strictly be interpreted as a reorganization procedure. However, the business as such, as distinct from the legal entity, may be reorganised upon the sale of the business by the administrator. A Receiver or a Receiver and Manager is usually appointed by a secured creditor to realize assets covered by the security when the debtor Company has made default under the terms of the security. The Receiver's primary function is to realize sufficient funds from the assets over which he is appointed to repay the debt owed to the secured creditor. A Receiver is commonly appointed under the terms of a debenture charge that extends over all the Company's assets and undertakings, and provides wide powers to deal with the assets and carry on the Company's business.

A Receiver may be appointed privately, by the Court, or as a result of statutory power (a rarity). The procedure for receivership is not statute defined but originates from the law of contract. However, a number of duties and obligations and powers are imposed and conferred by the Companies Code (Part X in particular), and by the various State Supreme Court Rules governing Court procedures.

Receivership may involve:

• Carrying on the Company's business.
• Winding up the Company's business affairs.
• Distributing corporate property to particular parties.
• An examination of trading performance and financial position.

Receivership may be instigated voluntarily by the Company itself or involuntarily by other parties who wish to force such an administration. The prime advantages of this form of administration, especially for private appointors, are the speed and simplicity of instigating the appointment and the minimal cost involved. A further advantage accruing after the appointment of a Receiver is to prevent unsecured creditors enforcing judgments against Company assets secured by the debenture holder. For those entities who have special rights or seek special protection, receivership provides an administration that will be tailored to their rights or requirements, rather than the interests of creditors as a whole. Hence, the administrator is afforded some flexibility.

Accordingly, the appointment of a Receiver does not necessarily protect the interests of ordinary creditors, and such creditors may choose to initiate an alternative insolvency administration, whether instead of or in addition to receivership.

2.3.1 Types of Appointment — The most common method to initiate a receivership is by private appointment pursuant to a debenture conferring a fixed or floating charge over the assets of a Company. The second form of appointment is by the Courts pursuant to their powers of jurisdiction.

(a) Private appointments are usually made pursuant to powers arising out of an express agreement between the parties interested in property over which the appointment is made, such as pursuant to a mortgage or debenture deed. Private appointments are also made less commonly, pursuant to statutory powers that appear in conveyancing and real property legislation of the Australian States.

Appointing a Receiver out of Court normally has the dual advantages of reduction of cost and legal formalities and quick achievement. Additionally, wider powers are conferred upon a Receiver/Receiver and Manager than under a Court appointment, whether by an original agreement with the Company or by reference to conveyancing legislation.

Conveyancing legislation permits a Receiver to be appointed privately under a mortgage deed that fails to provide for the appointment of a Receiver. It implies certain powers to a Receiver appointed pursuant to a mortgage deed when the deed is silent.

The use of appointments pursuant to conveyancing legislation has declined because:

- It is limited in the scope of the powers permitted to a Receiver.

- A statutory period may need to elapse before the appointment can be made.

- Lenders have become more sophisticated in settling their own contractual terms for the appointment of a Receiver.

- The Companies legislation imposing requirements on a Receiver now applies to a Receiver of a portion or of all Company property, so that one of the former advantages of making a Conveyancing Act appointment under a portion only of a Company's property is no longer available.

Private appointments may be initiated by persons having the right to do so under contract. The Company itself may request such parties to appoint a Receiver to effect an orderly insolvency administration.

(b) Court Appointments arise from the Court's jurisdiction to appoint a Receiver when it appears to the Court to be just or convenient to do so. Court Appointments may also arise from statutory powers outside the Supreme Court legislation, such as the Securities Industry Code or the Companies Code. Such appointments are rare.

Certain precedents have been set as to under what circumstances the Court believes it is just and convenient to appoint a Receiver. The appointment must not only be made because justice requires it, it must also be practicable. A Receiver may be appointed by the Court pending resolution of Court proceedings in the circumstances when an independent person is required to have receiving powers or when one of the parties is incompetent to 'receive.' The Receiver is usually appointed to take possession and control of, and manage (if necessary), property that is the subject of the dispute.

The appointment of a Court receiver is usually an interim measure made in a situation in which the applicant cannot appoint a Receiver privately.

A Court appointed Receiver therefore adopts a caretaker role, whereas a privately appointed Receiver attempts to restore the financial prosperity of the Company or repay a debenture holder.

2.3.2 Initiating the Appointment of a Receiver

(a) Appointment Under Powers Contained in a Debenture.

The procedure for initiating the appointment of a Receiver is usually contained in the original mortgage, debenture, or other contract giving rise to the power of appointment. The debenture contract should provide that the appointment of a Receiver is to be made in writing. Statute does not define any method of appointment.

The debenture should also provide for conditions under which a Receiver might be appointed such as repayment defaults or the insolvency of the borrower.

The debenture may provide that a formal demand for repayment be made and not met before a Receiver can be appointed. The appointment takes effect from the date when the Receiver is provided with his instrument of appointment by the lender and he accepts that appointment.

(b) Appointment Pursuant to Conveyancing (Real Property) Legislation.

Conveyancing legislation in each State grants certain powers to a mortgagee under a deed of mortgage, as if those powers were conferred by the actual deed. These powers include the power to appoint a Receiver of the mortgaged property or any part thereof.

Under the legislation, a Receiver can only be appointed after the statutory power of sale becomes exercisable, which in turn normally requires a lapse of time such as three months from the formal demand to repay. This is a shortcoming of the legislation that has resulted in its replacement by specific contractual powers. When timing is a material limitation, a lender may apply to the Court to appoint a Receiver.

(c) Appointment of a Court Receiver.

A Receiver may be appointed by the Court as an equitable remedy whenever it is just and convenient to do so. A Receiver can be sought by any party to a cause or matter involving the Court's jurisdiction. In practice, applicants are usually mortgagees, or debenture holders, although the appointment could be sought in unusual circumstances by ordinary creditors and even by the Company itself perhaps to resolve factional disputes.

The procedure for securing a Court order will depend upon the circumstances in which the order is sought.

A person who is appointed as, or acts as, a Receiver of Company property must be a registered liquidator pursuant to Section 323 of the Companies Code.

2.3.3 Receiver's Powers — The Receiver's most important initial task is to secure possession of the Company property which his appointment gives him the right to secure and, to the extent that it is necessary to do so, to assert his authority over the corporation. His prime duty when appointed by a debenture holder is that of repaying the debenture holder. To carry out this objective, a Receiver is normally given wide powers of realisation and of carrying on business. The Receiver is given power by statute to carry on business unless such power is excluded by the instrument of appointment (Section 324 A(2)(h) of the Companies Code).

A Court-appointed Receiver often has no power of sale, except with permission of the Court. The same can be said of a Receiver appointed under conveyancing legislation.

The Receiver's powers to administer corporate property are somewhat circumscribed by the terms of his appointment. However, he is assisted by Section 324A of the Companies Code, which provides a Receiver with a range of powers to be available wherever required in connection with or incidental to the attainment of the objectives for which the Receiver was appointed.

A Receiver also has power to investigate a Company's affairs and to report to the Commission on possible corporate offences pursuant to Section 324C of the Companies Code.

The nature of the Receiver's authority and the extent of his powers are derived from the contract between the parties, the appointment document, the Court order (where applicable), and the requirements imposed by the Companies Code, and where relevant, conveyancing legislation. A privately appointed Receiver is usually the agent of the mortgagor Company, as deemed by conventional agreements and conveyancing legislation.

Any Receiver who enters into possession or assumes control of Company property for the purpose of enforcing a charge is personally liable for debts incurred by him during the course of the receivership. However, the Receiver has a right of indemnity from Company property.

Conversely, a Court-appointed Receiver is an officer of the Court responsible to discharge certain duties prescribed by the order appointing him until that appointment is revoked. The duty of a Court-appointed Receiver will depend on the purpose of his appointment and the scope of the Court order.

2.3.4 Receiver's Obligations — Although the Receiver may be an agent of the Company and have certain duties in relation to the Company, his prime responsibility will not be to the Company, but to the persons or the Court appointing him. Under a private appointment, based upon contractual powers, this prime responsibility is inevitably owed to a lender/supplier who is entitled to repayment under the debenture contract. This is a unique feature of receivership, separating it from other insolvency administrations where the administrator owes his prime responsibility to creditors in general. A Receiver is not obliged to report to individual creditors nor to consult with them.

Upon appointment, the Receiver must advise the Company in writing of his appointment, and lodge statutory documents giving notification of his appointment with the Corporate Affairs Commission and the Deputy Commissioner of Taxation. He must also open a separate bank account, visit all locations of trading and secure all assets, obtain insurance cover on tangible assets, offer reemployment to necessary staff, and anything else that is necessary to protect the interests of the appointor.

A Report or Statement of Affairs document as at the date of appointment must be obtained from the present and/or former Company officers and filed with the Commissioner for Corporate Affairs, together with any comments thereon. The progress of the Receivership should also be regularly reported to the debenture holder/Court and the Company's affairs should be investigated to determine if the Directors have been guilty of an offence.

A receiver is not liable for prereceivership debts nor other contractual obligations arising after the date of appointment, provided he does not adopt that contract. However, a Receiver is personally liable for goods and services supplied to the Company under his authorization.

The net proceeds obtained from trading or from the sale of Company assets, after deducting receivership fees and expenses, must be apportioned between fixed and floating charge assets.

Proceeds derived from assets subject to a specific fixed charge may be applied in favor of the debenture holder as no other creditors are afforded a higher priority, assuming control of all the Company's property does not pass to the Receiver. If control of all a Company's property were to pass to a Receiver appointed under a fixed charge, then unremitted group tax deductions, prescribed payments, tax deductions, and withholding tax deductions would rank in priority to payments to the debenture holder; although such an occurrence would be unusual and would apply where a Company had, for example, only one form of asset, such as debtors, in its balance sheet. However, prior to repaying the holder of a floating charge, the Receiver must first satisfy the claims of preferential creditors as prescribed by the Companies Code, the Income Tax Assessment Act, and the Court Order or Debenture Agreement. These preferential claims include the following, listed in descending order of priority:

- Unremitted Group Tax and Prescribed Payments Tax deductions (from employee wages and contract labor payments), and Withholding Tax Deductions.
- Rents, taxes, rates, and outgoings affecting the property in question.
- Costs, charges, and expenses incurred by the Receiver.
- Receiver's remuneration.
- Net proceeds of insurance against third party liabilities to be applied to the person injured or affected.
- Fees and expenses of an auditor who had applied to the Corporate Affairs Commission before the date of receivership for resignation as an auditor, or whose application to resign is refused by the Commission. This priority also applies to an auditor who makes application after the receivership but only in respect of fees and expenses incurred after the Commission's refusal to accept that resignation.
- Employee wages up to a limit of $2,000 in respect of services rendered prior to receivership.
- All amounts due prior to receivership to an employee in respect of leave of absence (long service leave, extended leave, recreation leave, annual leave or sick leave) by virtue of an industrial instrument. This should not exceed $1,500 in respect of an excluded employee (i.e., a director, his or her spouse, or a relative of a director).
- Retrenchment payments payable to employees other than 'excluded employees.'
- Repayments to Debenture Holder.
- Payment of any surplus to those entitled to receive it, whether it be a subsequent encumbrancer, a Liquidator, or the Company itself.

In a Court-appointed receivership, the plaintiff's costs of action will be accorded some ranking in the above order of priority in advance of priority creditors and repayments to debenture holders.

2.3.5 Termination of the Receivership — After the Receiver has discharged his receivership duties and liabilities and completed his administration formalities and objectives, he is then in a position to terminate the receivership and retire as Receiver and Manager or be discharged.

Prior to resigning or applying for a discharge, and, if possible, prior to the debenture holder discharging the Receiver, the Receiver should ensure that he has:

- Realized all property of the Company available to him, or so much of the property as is required to repay the debenture holder.
- Repaid or allowed for all of his costs and expenses and for creditors required to be paid in priority to the debenture holder.

- Informed relevant parties of the impending termination of the receivership.

When a receivership is terminated, the Company's existence continues and control of any remaining property reverts to its Directors, unless a Liquidator or other Administrator is acting, or the Receiver is replaced.

Where a Receiver is removed, resigns, or dies, the receivership may continue if a replacement is made within a reasonable time.

The Receiver must notify the Commissioner of Corporate Affairs that he has ceased to act.

B. Partnerships, Joint Debtors and Individuals

The primary reorganization procedures applicable to unincorporated businesses and private individuals, be they traders or nontraders, are:

- Deed of Assignment
- Composition
- Deed of Arrangement
- Informal Arrangements
- Noncorporate Receivership

All the above reorganization procedures, with the exception of noncorporate receivership and informal arrangements, are arrangements or agreements made between a debtor and his creditors pursuant to Part X of the Bankruptcy Act, 1966. They are known as 'Part X Arrangements.' They are statute defined procedures giving sanction to such arrangements. A Part X Arrangement originates in a proposal by a debtor to his creditors, and is binding on all creditors if a meeting of creditors (the proposal meeting) agrees by special resolution to accept it. The debtor must voluntarily initiate the convening of the meeting by giving written authority to a registered trustee or a solicitor.

In effect, Part X permits debtors and creditors to determine how a debtor's affairs should be administered outside the rigid code of bankruptcy. If a debtor's proposal is accepted and he enters into a Part X Arrangement, creditors appoint a trustee to act on their behalf to realize assets, collect moneys payable, and pay dividends. The trustee must be a registered trustee.

Part X of the Bankruptcy Act provides the procedure by which noncorporate debtors and creditors may reach arrangements that:

- Avoid bankruptcy, and with it the need for a creditor to force a sequestration order.
- Retain many of the requirements and protections of the Bankruptcy Act, including the appointment of a trustee to look after the interests of creditors and pay equitable dividends.
- Provide relief to the debtor so that he may continue to start afresh.
- Are binding on the debtor and his creditors.

- Can be simply initiated without recourse to the Court -- although documents initiating a Part X Arrangement must be filed with the Registrar in Bankruptcy.

Part X also provides for an optional interim administration referred to as a 'controlling trusteeship,' which commences when and if the debtor requests a registered trustee to convene a meeting of creditors to consider his proposal and to take control of his property.

A controlling trusteeship ceases when an arrangement becomes effective or is rejected. If a solicitor is appointed to convene the proposal meeting, there will be no independent control of the debtor's property prior to the meeting.

An arrangement occurs when a meeting of creditors accepts a composition by a debtor, or the debtor executes a Deed of Assignment or Deed of Arrangement as required by the proposal meeting.

Arrangements are more likely to include substantial assets than are bankruptcies.

In Noncorporate Receiverships, a secured creditor is commonly secured to a fixed or identifiable asset, and receivership commonly arises from a dispute with a receiver being appointed by the Court. A Receiver is often appointed, especially in partnership cases, with a view to winding up the business as his limited powers often restrict the carrying on of business of the debtor. A noncorporate receiver is only required to report to the Court. The Companies Code does not impose obligations on a noncorporate receiver.

2.4 Deed of Assignment — A Deed of Assignment is a means by which all of a debtor's divisible property, with the exception of after-acquired property (property that is acquired after the execution of the Deed) is assigned to a trustee for the benefit of his creditors. The debtor divests himself of all property that would have been available to or recoverable by a trustee in bankruptcy. This form of arrangement is most like bankruptcy. Upon execution of an assignment, a debtor is released from all provable debts and he is under no continuing disability.

A trustee also has powers similar to a bankruptcy trustee, including the power to recover assets by operation of relation back, voidable settlement, and voidable preference principles.

A Deed of Assignment is initiated by a debtor's authority given under Section 188 of the Bankruptcy Act to a registered trustee or solicitor, who must then convene a meeting of creditors. A statement of the debtor's affairs must be presented to the creditors' meeting. The creditors must agree by special resolution to sanction an agreement. Creditors agree to require execution of a deed by a debtor, which, when executed, commences the administration and binds creditors.

A trustee must be elected and act for all creditors. He is appointed if a meeting of creditors sanctions the arrangement, and may be removed by a special resolution of creditors.

The trustee is vested with the debtor's assets but is restricted in carrying on business except for the beneficial disposal of assets or the winding up of the business.

A Deed of Assignment precludes property acquired after the date of the Deed's execution being available to creditors and creditors are repaid in the same priorities as in bankruptcy. As in bankruptcy, there is a requirement to investigate for the potential recovery of assets and to report to creditors. There is provision for an optional examination of the debtor, if necessary.

When there is no creditor animosity toward the debtor, a Deed of Assignment may be appropriate, particularly when there is no desire by the debtor, or it is not viable, to carry on business and the debtor cannot afford to make, or creditors do not seek, future repayments.

A trustee's function is to realize the debtor's divisible property, investigate the causes of insolvency and recover whatever assets would have been available in bankruptcy with the exception of any property acquired after the date of execution of the deed.

If creditors are prepared to let the debtor avoid bankruptcy, yet wish to preserve all the investigating and recovery powers available to a trustee in bankruptcy, with the exception of access to after-acquired income or property, then a Deed of Assignment is the appropriate administration.

2.5 Composition — A Composition is an arrangement by which creditors agree to accept less than what is due to them in relation to the amount and/or timing of payment of their debt in full satisfaction of their debt. A Composition, which may be a deed or a mere proposal, is an offer by a debtor to his creditors that fully satisfies the debts owed. The acceptance of a Composition by creditors releases the debtor immediately from his provable debts. The terms of the Composition must be specified in the resolution accepting it, and the resolution must be lodged with the Registrar in Bankruptcy.

A Composition is initiated by an authority given by a debtor under Section 188 of the Bankruptcy Act to a registered trustee or a solicitor who must then convene a meeting of creditors. If the authority is given to a trustee, all the debtor's property becomes subject to control by him as controlling trustee pending the determination of the creditors meeting. A Statement of Affairs must be presented to the creditors meeting.

Creditors must agree by special resolution to accept a Composition which then commences and becomes binding on creditors. As with other Part X Arrangements, a Trustee is elected by the creditors if the Composition proposal is accepted. The Trustee's fees require approval from a creditors meeting or the Court. As there is no formal Committee of Inspection in a Composition, such a Committee would have no authority to approve remuneration.

Under a Composition, the trustee's control over the debtor's assets will usually consist of no more than collecting repayments from the debtor to allow dividends to be paid to creditors. Only the assets promised by the Composition are available for distribution to creditors, and the priority of creditor repayments is not necessarily the same as in bankruptcy. The function of the Trustee is to act as an intermediary between the debtor and his creditors by collecting promised receipts from the debtor and making dispositions to the creditors and reporting to them accordingly. There is no provision in the Bankruptcy Act that allows a Trustee of a Composition to recover further assets than promised in the Composition, and he is not empowered to conduct an examination of the debtor.

A Composition will be the most appropriate form of administration of an individual debtor in the following circumstances:

(i) When there are few or no assets available other than future repayments from the debtor. This may sway creditors away from the pursuit of bankruptcy proceedings.

(ii) When the debtor's business is required to continue to fund repayments, but it is not of a kind that could be supervised economically by a trustee.

(iii) When creditors accept that partial payment is the only way to permit the debtor a fresh start with sufficient financial capacity and incentive to succeed.

The extent to which a debt will be compromised will depend upon the debtor's available assets and expected earnings and the creditors' desire to see the debtor continue his business or avoid bankruptcy. A Composition is usually the least supervised of all arrangements as the trustee normally merely performs a collection and distribution function.

2.6 Deed of Arrangement — A Deed of Arrangement provides for an arrangement to repay debts, in whole or in part, by a method other than prescribed by a Deed of Assignment or a Composition. Such a Deed can be formulated to suit the circumstances and may range from a supervised moratorium, where debts are ultimately paid in full, to an arrangement to carry on business providing for repayment only if profits are earned, or there may be a scheme to generate moneys combined with a minimum dividend requirement or arrangements involving contributions, guarantees, or securities from third parties. A Deed of Arrangement may even consist of an assignment of assets combined with additional undertakings to repay from future income.

As long as a Deed of Arrangement does not interfere with the guidelines provided by the Bankruptcy Act, it will be permissible.

Under a Deed of Arrangement, debts are only released to the extent specified in the Deed itself.

As with other Part X Arrangements, a Deed of Arrangement is initiated by a Debtor's authority given under Section 188 of the Bankruptcy Act to a registered Trustee or a solicitor, who then is required to call a meeting of creditors. If creditors agree by special resolution to sanction a Deed, the administration commences when the Deed is executed.

Under a Deed of Arrangement, the degree of a Trustee's control of a Debtor's assets will be determined by the terms of the Deed itself, and only the assets specified in the Deed are available for distribution. Debts are usually repaid in the same priorities as in bankruptcy; however, this may be expanded by the Deed. An optional examination of the debtor is available under a Deed of Arrangement in relation to his acts and dealings and the discovery of undeclared property.

A Deed of Arrangement may be appropriate where arrangements to satisfy creditors are detailed. A Deed of Arrangement may consist of part compromise and part assignment, or continued supervision of the Debtor's business by the Trustee, or measurement of the Debtor's performance. It is most likely to be utilized when there is some prospect of trading out of financial difficulties. It is a flexible agreement similar to a corporate scheme of arrangement, which may be tailored to measure. Assets that would be available in bankruptcy or under a Deed of Assignment may be made available under a Deed of Arrangement (i.e., all divisible assets may be assigned), and further contributions (e.g., from future income) may be promised by the Debtor). A Deed may also require a Debtor to make fixed repayments on specified dates; or to assign certain assets to the Trustee for sale and distribution to creditors; or to carry on business under the control of the Trustee with periodic dividends to be paid out of profits.

If the terms of a Deed are not adhered to by a Debtor, Creditors may terminate the Deed.

2.7 Informal Arrangements — Informal arrangements or schemes may be proposed by a debtor seeking to defer repayments to creditors due to liquidity problems; at the same time he may seek continued credit to enable the continuation of business or completion of work in progress.

However, although such arrangements are agreed to by creditors, they are difficult to enforce compared with formal arrangements, and may be voided by Part X of the Bankruptcy Act if they are not in compliance with the Part of the Act.

2.8 Noncorporate Receiverships — Noncorporate Receiverships are similar to Corporate Receiverships in principle and we will not dwell on this form of administration too much except to distinguish it from Corporate Receivership.

Commonly, the purpose of a noncorporate receivership appointment is to resolve a partnership dispute, or to distribute partnership assets. In a noncorporate receivership, the debtor is usually a sole-proprietor or partnership, and occasionally may be a club or other form of organization consisting of a group of members. A secured creditor is usually secured to a fixed or identifiable asset, and the appointment commonly involves winding up the business undertaking due to the limited powers of a receiver in a noncorporate appointment with regard to trading on the debtor's business. A Receiver appointed over a noncorporate debtor's property may need only account to Court if he is appointed by the Court; otherwise, there are no formal reporting requirements by the Receiver as the National Companies Code is not relevant.

Unlike other noncorporate insolvency administrations such as bankruptcy or a Part X Arrangement in which the administrator's prime responsibility is to creditors in general, the receiver's prime responsibility is to the persons or the Court appointing him. Accordingly, a receivership and bankruptcy administration may occur simultaneously.

3. TERMINAL PROCEDURES

Terminal procedures are methods by which limited companies, partnerships, joint debtors, and individuals have their assets realized and their affairs wound up. As with reorganization procedures, terminal procedures for limited companies differ from those applicable to partnerships, joint debtors, and individuals.

A. Limited Companies

There are three modes of liquidation, these are as follows:

(a) Members' Voluntary Liquidation.

(b) Creditors' Voluntary Liquidation.

(c) Court Liquidation.

Members' Voluntary Liquidations are applicable to solvent companies, whereas Creditors' Voluntary and Court Liquidations are utilized to terminate insolvent companies.

3.1 Members' Voluntary Liquidation — The purpose of a Members' Voluntary Liquidation is to enable a solvent Company to wind up its affairs and to provide a fair and equitable distribution of the Company's surplus assets among its members after repaying all outstanding liabilities. A members' voluntary liquidation can only be instigated if, pursuant to Section 392 of the Companies Code, the members of a corporation agree voluntarily by a 75% majority (a special resolution) to wind up the affairs of the Company. If such a majority cannot agree, then an application may be made to the Court for an order to wind up the Company.

If during the course of a members' voluntary liquidation it becomes apparent to the Liquidator that the Company is not solvent, the Liquidator must take steps to convert the liquidation to a creditors' voluntary liquidation. A members' voluntary liquidation is conducted by a liquidator who is elected and controlled by the shareholders.

A Liquidator must consent to act prior to his appointment, and he need not be a Registered Liquidator if the Company is an exempt proprietary company or a subsidiary of a public Company. However, a registered liquidator is generally used in practice.

3.1.1 Commencement of Proceedings — The initiation of a member's voluntary liquidation involves the following:

(a) Firstly, a Meeting of Directors must be called and held to consider the placement of the Company into liquidation. At this Meeting, a Declaration of Solvency must be made and signed pursuant to Section 395 of the Companies Code, and a Consent to Act as Liquidator must be tabled from the prospective Liquidator. Attached to the Declaration of Solvency is a Statement of the Company's Affairs, which should illustrate the Company's solvency (i.e., assets greater than liabilities). At this Meeting, the Directors resolve that the Company should call a Meeting of Members to resolve that the Company be wound up voluntarily and that a particular Liquidator be appointed for such purpose.

(b) Subsequent to the Directors' Meeting, the Declaration of Solvency (Companies Form 97) must be lodged at the Corporate Affairs Commission (usually the same or next day). After this form is lodged, the Secretary then forwards a Notice of Extraordinary General Meeting (EGM) to the Members/Shareholders of the Company.

(c) If less than three weeks notice is to be given for calling the Extraordinary General Meeting, it is necessary for a majority in number of members, who hold 95% in nominal value of the shares representing not less than 95% of the total voting rights of all Members having the right to attend and vote at the Meeting, to agree to short notice being given. If there is no such agreement, a special resolution cannot be proposed or passed at the Meeting (EGM). This agreement may be given by the signing of an Authority for calling Short Notice of Extraordinary General Meeting prior to the Meeting. Therefore the EGM may be held within a few days of the Notice of EGM being sent out.

(d) At the Extraordinary General meeting of Members, it is resolved that the Company be wound up voluntarily and that a Liquidator be appointed for that purpose. The scale of the Liquidator's remuneration is also approved by the Meeting.

(e) Subsequent to the Meeting, a copy of the minutes together with a Notice of Resolution (Companies Form 24) and a Notice of Appointment of Liquidator (Companies Form 102) are lodged at the Corporate Affairs Commission and a Notice is placed in the Commonwealth Government Gazette advertising the Company's placement into liquidation and giving notice to creditors that they must furnish particulars of their claims to the Liquidator within 21 days.

    The Liquidator then forwards correspondence to the relevant tax authorities and closes the Company's bank account(s) and opens a Liquidator's bank account with these funds. The liquidation can then proceed in its normal course.

3.1.2 Liquidator's Duties — After appointment the duties of the Liquidator include:

- Realizing the assets of the Company.
- Discharging all the liabilities of the Company.
- Lodging six-monthly accounts of receipts and payments (Companies Form 106) with the Corporate Affairs Commission.
- If the administration continues for more than one year, convening annual general meetings of shareholders within three months of the anniversary date for the purpose of reporting on the conduct and progress of the liquidation.
- Depositing all funds into a Liquidator's account.
- Distribution of surplus funds to beneficial shareholders in accordance with the rights attached to class of share as prescribed by the Memorandum and Articles of Association.

3.1.3 Creditors' Position — In a members' voluntary liquidation, the Company should pay all creditors in full, as the Company should be solvent. Accordingly the priority of creditors is irrelevant, except with regard to the timing of repayments and the pressure exerted by certain creditors for payment. In circumstances in which, due to the insolvency of a Company, it is converted from a members' voluntary to a creditors' voluntary liquidation, the priorities of repayment are governed by the Companies Code. These priorities are detailed in the creditors' voluntary liquidation Section of this Guide.

Although Section 395(1) of the Companies Code requires the Directors to declare that the Company will be able to pay its debts in full within a period not exceeding 12 months after the commencement of the winding up, frequently this may be frustrated by the Deputy Commissioner of Taxation who may extend the length of an administration due to delays in obtaining a claim or clearance from his office.

In a members' voluntary winding up, all debts payable on a contingency and all claims against the Company are admissible to prove against the Company, a just estimate being made so far as possible of the value of such debts or claims as are subject to any contingency or do not bear a certain value. This is in contrast to the liquidation of an insolvent Company, where more stringent rules apply.

As creditors have no say in their selection of the Liquidator, their only remedy, should they believe their rights are being prejudiced, is to apply to the Court for a compulsory winding up.

3.1.4 Shareholders' Position — After the Liquidator has fulfilled his duties of realizing all assets and paying creditors' claims and the costs of the winding up, he is then in a position to distribute any surplus assets to the shareholders according to their rights and interests in the Company as specified in the Company's Articles of Association.

Distributions to shareholders are not subject to taxation deductions by the Liquidator, unless shareholders reside overseas, which would require a Liquidator to deduct withholding tax from that portion of the distribution represented by unappropriated profits. The Articles of Association usually permit the Liquidator to distribute or transfer the surplus assets in specie (in kind) or in cash to the beneficial shareholders.

Normally, after the commencement of the winding up, several months will elapse before the Liquidator can make a final distribution to the beneficial shareholders. The delay is due primarily to the Taxation Commissioner being slow in providing the liquidator with a Taxation Clearance. However, if an indemnity is received by the Liquidator from either shareholders or an associated party for the payment of outstanding income tax or other liabilities that may arise, then the liquidation process may be hastened as the Liquidator is then able to proceed with the distribution of the surplus assets to the beneficial shareholders prior to the determination of whether any outstanding taxation is due. Despite this, the Final Meeting of Members cannot be called until all liabilities have been dispensed with. Therefore, a Taxation Clearance is also required for this purpose.

3.1.5 Termination of the Winding up — Upon finalization of the above matters, the Liquidator can then proceed to terminate the winding up by calling a Final Meeting of Members of the Company. In this regard, one month's Notice is required to be given both by post to the Members and by Notice issued in the Commonwealth Government Gazette. At this Final Meeting, the Liquidator furnishes an account of the Conduct of the Winding Up and a Statement of his Acts and Dealings.

At the conclusion of the Final meeting, the Liquidator is required to lodge a Final Account of Receipts and Payments (Companies Form 106) and a Return by Liquidator relating to Final Meeting (Companies Form 100), with an Account of the Conduct of the Winding Up attached, with the Commissioner for Corporate Affairs. Details of any distributions to Company members are also required to be furnished with the Deputy Commissioner of Taxation. Three months after the Final Meeting, the Company is officially 'dissolved' and is struck off the Companies Register at the Corporate Affairs Commission.

The Commissioner of Corporate Affairs has power pursuant to Section 459 of the Companies Code to remove a defunct Company (which has no assets or liabilities) from the Company Register, without regard to the process of liquidation. In this regard, a voluntary application may be made by the Company to the Commissioner requesting that he exercise his power to deregister the Company, thereby foregoing the fees and expenses of a liquidator in the winding-up process.

3.2 Creditors' Voluntary Liquidation — An insolvent Company that wishes to wind up its affairs voluntarily without application to the Court must follow the procedure of a creditors' voluntary winding up. A creditors' voluntary winding up is initiated by the Directors and Shareholders who must resolve by special resolution to wind up the Company's affairs voluntarily. A creditors' meeting is then held immediately, this gives creditors the opportunity to replace the Liquidator nominated by members. A creditors' voluntary winding up is conducted by a Liquidator under the ultimate control of creditors. Its purpose is to wind up the affairs of a corporation voluntarily and to provide a fair and equitable distribution to the corporation's property among creditors.

3.2.1 Commencement of Proceedings — The following procedures are necessary to instigate a creditors' voluntary liquidation:

(a) Directors should hold a meeting to resolve that the Company be wound up voluntarily if they are of the opinion that the Company cannot pay its debts as and when they fall due and there is no reason to believe that the Company will regain solvency. At this meeting, the Directors resolve that meetings of shareholders and creditors be convened for the purpose of placing the Company into liquidation and appointing a Liquidator.

Usually, Directors approach an insolvency practitioner (the potential Liquidator) for initial advice, and a letter of authority is obtained by him to act on behalf of the Company in calling the meetings of members and creditors and assisting directors in preparing a Report as to Affairs of the Company.

(b) Notices in writing must be given for the meetings of members and creditors and the creditors' meeting must be advertised.

(c) A consent to short notice of the members' meeting may be obtained from 95% of shareholders prior to the members' meeting in order that less than three weeks notice be given.

(d) The Notice of Creditors' Meeting must be accompanied by a Summary of the Company's Affairs, a list of creditors, a proof of debt form, and a Proxy form. At least seven days clear notice must be given.

(e) The Creditors' Meeting must be advertised in a daily newspaper not more than 14 days prior to the meeting and not less than seven days prior to the meeting.

(f) A copy of the Notice to Creditors and the Summary of Affairs must be lodged prior to the Creditors' Meeting.

(g) A complete report as to the Company's affairs document must be prepared prior to the Creditors' Meeting to be tabled at that Meeting.

3.2.2 Shareholders' Meeting — Creditors themselves cannot instigate a voluntary winding up. Their rights come into existence only when the Company takes steps to wind up voluntarily by calling a meeting of the Company members to pass a resolution to this effect. Section 398 of the Companies Code sets out the procedure for this. This Section provides that the Company shall cause a meeting of its creditors to be summoned for the day, or for the following day, on which the members' meeting is to be held to consider a resolution for winding up. A special resolution is required at the meeting of members to place the Company into voluntary liquidation. From that point in time, the Company is in liquidation. If the requisite majority of members do not resolve to place the Company into voluntary liquidation, the only course open to creditors is to apply for a winding-up order.

The nomination of a Liquidator by shareholders may be ratified by creditors or they may overrule the shareholders' decision and appoint a Liquidator of their own nomination. If creditors cannot agree who will act as Liquidator, the Liquidator appointed by shareholders will remain in office. Pursuant to Section 248 of the Companies Code, 21 days' notice is required to convene the meeting of members unless at least 95% of members agree to short notice being given. However, as the Code requires notice of the creditors' meeting to be sent out simultaneously with notices of the meeting of members, and as the meeting of creditors must be preceded by at least seven clear days' notice, it follows that at least seven days clear notice must be given for the members' meeting.

3.2.3 Creditors' Meeting — The meeting of creditors must be convened at a time and place convenient to the majority in value of the creditors, and must be preceded by at least seven days clear notice sent by post to every creditor. The notice must be accompanied by a Summary of Affairs document, together with a list of creditors showing their names, addresses, and amounts due; a Proof of Debt form; and a Proxy form. A copy of the notice of the meeting must be published in a daily newspaper circulating generally throughout the State or Territory at least seven days and not more than fourteen days before the date of the meeting. Failure to advertise the meeting is not necessarily fatal to the validity of the proceedings, but it will have this consequence if the absence of notice results in substantial injustice.

At the creditors' meeting, the Directors must cause to be laid before the meeting a report in the prescribed form, and verified by all Directors, as to the affairs of the Company. One of the Directors and the Secretary must attend the meeting to disclose to the meeting the Company's affairs and report on the circumstances leading to the proposed winding up of the Company. Usually the meeting is opened by the convening accountant (i.e., the proposed Liquidator) and a Chairman is elected by the meeting. The Chairman may be a Director, a creditor, their proxy (commonly a solicitor or professional accountant), or the convening accountant provided he does not use proxies in his favor to vote himself into a position of remuneration (Liquidator). It is the Chairman's duty to determine whether the meeting has been held at a date, time, and place convenient to the majority in value of creditors. His decision on the matter is final and if he decides that the time and place are not convenient, the meeting lapses and the Company must summon a further meeting as soon as practicable.

At the meeting, creditors nominate a person to act as liquidator, and if their choice differs from that of the shareholders, their nomination prevails. Ordinarily, the remuneration of the Liquidator is fixed by the creditors' meeting; however, if a committee of inspection is appointed, it determines the Liquidator's remuneration.

Any creditor, other than one whose debt is unliquidated or contingent, may vote at the meeting provided that he has lodged with the Chairman a proof of the debt that he claims is due to him and provided, in the case of a secured creditor, that he values his security in his proof and votes only in respect of the balance over and above that value.

3.2.4 Liquidator — In a creditors' voluntary winding up, the Liquidator must be a registered Liquidator with the Corporate Affairs Commission. The appointed Liquidator must first have consented in writing to act should he be nominated, and he must advertise his appointment.

The Liquidator's most important initial task is to identify and secure possession of the Company's assets and attempt to obtain and/or inspect the Company's records at an early stage. An inventory of physical assets may be required and/or expert evaluations may have to be arranged by the Liquidator. Assets must be insured unless existing insurances are adequate.

Additional property may be recovered by the application of offence provisions of the Companies Code, or its various recovery provisions, which include setting aside invalid charges and the recovery of preferential payments or voidable dispositions.

The Liquidator must form a strategy for the realization of assets to provide the most beneficial return for creditors. This may involve carrying on business to complete work in progress, to obtain market values for stock, or to enable the sale of the business as a going concern. However, the Companies Code (Section 394) only permits a Liquidator to carry on business for the beneficial disposal or winding up of that business.

Unlike the situation in a Court liquidation, a voluntary Liquidator requires no authority of the Court, creditors, or a Committee to carry on business for such beneficial winding up.

The employment of previous management and selling agents may be necessary to realize Company assets.

The Liquidator has the responsibility to ascertain the assets and liabilities of the Company, and he should report on matters of interest to creditors or members, or that in his opinion he ought to bring to the notice of the Commission. Section 418 of the Companies Code requires a Liquidator to report to the Commission if he has found evidence of the following:

- An offence by persons connected with the Company;
- Misapplication or misuse of corporate funds or property;
- Negligence, default, breach of duty, or breach of trust in relation to the Company;

or

- If the Company will be unable to pay its unsecured creditors more than 50 cents on the dollar.

These factors require a Liquidator to conduct an investigation into the affairs of the Company. The Liquidator will look for any unusual events, offences, or transactions that might give rise to potential claims or asset recoveries.

A Liquidator may elect to publicly examine any person connected or concerned with the affairs of the Company. The examination is commonly used to seek evidence in relation to a potential recovery or litigation. The transcript of the examination may be used as evidence in proceedings against the examinee.

A Liquidator has power to convene meetings of creditors. He must summon a meeting whenever he wishes to report to creditors at first hand, to consult formally with them, or to appoint a Committee of Inspection of creditors to assist him.

He must convene annual meetings of creditors and a final meeting of creditors when the affairs of the Company are fully wound up. A Liquidator will normally convene a meeting of the Committee of Inspection to secure approval for his remuneration. Whether the Liquidator convenes meetings of creditors or of the Committee or not, he should report in writing the following:

- Details of the Company's property and likely dividend distribution.
- The conduct of the Liquidator's administration.
- The circumstances leading to the liquidation and any important discoveries regarding the conduct, dealings, or transactions of the Company or its affairs.

The Liquidator must keep proper records and minutes of proceedings of meetings to give a complete and correct record of his administration. Any creditor may inspect these records.

Accounts of receipts and payments must be filed with the Commission within one month after the expiration of each six-month period during which he acts as Liquidator, and within one month of ceasing to act. A summary of the estimated position in the winding up must accompany this account.

A further requirement is for the Liquidator to maintain a special bank account, and invest surplus funds.

3.2.5 Committee of Inspection — To avoid the calling of a general meeting of creditors each time a Liquidator requires assistance on certain administrative matters, a Committee of Inspection may be appointed consisting of representatives of creditors and contributories. The task of the Committee is to supervise and assist the Liquidator in the performance of his duties and to watch over the interests of particular groups of creditors or contributories whom they are appointed to represent. There is no prescribed upper limit on the number of Committee members; however, the Companies Code requires a minimum of two members--otherwise the Committee cannot act.

Committee members occupy a fiduciary position in relation to the creditors and contributories that prevents them from deriving a profit from their office or from allowing their private interest to conflict with their duty as Committee members.

The Committee has a number of administrative duties, such as settling the remuneration of the Liquidator, but in practice it functions more as a consultative body than as an administrative or supervisory body. The Committee provides a useful forum to which the Liquidator can turn for advice and guidance on questions of policy. However, the Committee does exert some control over the Liquidator by virtue of its power to grant or withhold approval for the exercise of some of the Liquidator's powers, including his power to carry on business, to pay any class of creditor in full, and to reach a compromise with creditors or debtors of the Company.

In addition, in administering the assets of the Company, the Liquidator is bound to have regard to the directions of the Committee, although where he disagrees with their advice he may refer the matter to creditors and contributories at a general meeting, and their directions override those of the Committee. Alternatively, he may apply to the Court for directions.

3.2.6 Creditors' Position — When a sufficient fund of assets has been collected and realized, the Liquidator may begin the task of discharging the liabilities of the Company. The general rule, as embodied in Section 403 of the Companies Code, and applicable to both voluntary and compulsory winding up, is that the property of the Company is to be applied in satisfaction of its liabilities equally. The Companies Code (Section 440) provides that "except as otherwise provided by this Code, all debts proved in a winding up rank equally and, if the property of the Company is insufficient to meet them in full, they shall be paid proportionately." It is not uncommon in a liquidation that the exceptions have the effect of outweighing the rule. That is, special priority creditors frequently exhaust available assets.

Section 441 of the Companies Code is the principal source of statutory priorities in winding up; however, these priorities themselves are subject to priorities prescribed by the Income Tax Assessment Act. Not until all priority debts have been fully discharged or provided for to the specified extent may the Liquidator begin to apply the assets in payment of claims of unpreferred creditors, and, in the event that the Company's property is insufficient to meet a class of preferred debts in full, all debts in that class rank equally between themselves and each must suffer proportional abatement.

All claims must be agreed by reference to the amount due at the date the Company was placed into liquidation.

(A) PRIORITY OF CLAIMS

The following priorities apply in a Creditors' Voluntary Liquidation:

(i)   Secured Creditors from the proceeds of any fixed charged security, such as a real property mortgage, a registered bill of sale, or an assignment of trade debtors.

(ii)   Amounts due to the Deputy Commissioner of Taxation for unpaid income tax or sales tax from debtors to whom have been issued notices by the Commissioner pursuant to Section 218 of the Income Tax Assessment Act or Section 38 of the Sales Tax Act.

(iii)   The costs charges and expenses of winding up including the Liquidator's remuneration. In a compulsory winding up, this includes the taxed costs of a petitioning creditor/applicant for the winding up.

(iv)   Unremitted employee PAYE (Pay-As-You-Earn) Group Tax Deductions, or Prescribed Payments (PPS) tax deductions, or withholding tax deductions under the Income Tax Assessment Act, Section 221P, 221YHJ, 221YHZD, and 221YU.

(v)   If the winding up was preceded by the appointment of a provisional Liquidator — his reasonable costs charges, expenses, and remuneration.

(vi)   Where the winding up commences within two months after a period of official management:

   (a) The reasonable costs, charges, expenses and remuneration of the Official Manager, including the remuneration of any auditor.

   (b) Company debts properly and reasonably incurred by the Official Manager in carrying on business.

(vii)   Wages due to employees, but not exceeding $2,000 in respect of an excluded employee (i.e. a director, his spouse, or a relative of his).

(viii) All amounts due in respect of injury compensation.

(ix)   All amounts due to an employee in respect of leave of absence being amounts due by virtue of an industrial instrument (i.e., Holiday Pay, Long Service Leave, Leave in Lieu of Notice). Excluded Employees are limited to $1,500 as a priority.

(x)   Retrenchment payments payable to employees of the Company, other than excluded employees.

(xi)   (a) All municipal or other local rates outstanding at the liquidation date, which accrued within the 12 months preceding that date.

   (b) All amounts of income tax assessed under any State or Territory law (other than the Australian Capital Territory), but not exceeding one-year's assessment.

   (c) All amounts of land tax that were assessed under any State or Territory law (other than the A.C.T.), but not exceeding one year's assessment.

   (d) All amounts of payroll tax (other than payroll tax imposed by an Act of the Commonwealth) that were due and payable at the date of liquidation.

(e) All amounts that were due and payable at the date of liquidation:

   (i)   by way of repayment of any advance made to the company; or

   (ii) in respect of goods supplied or services rendered to the company,

   under any Act or Act of any other State or law of a Territory, other than the Australian Capital Territory, relating to or providing for the improvement, development, or settlement of land or the aid development or encouragement of mining;

   Where the Company has given security for the payment of the above rates, taxes, and amounts, they are to be preferred only if a balance is still owing after deducting the net proceeds realized from the security (Section 449).

(xii) Any amount pursuant to an order under Section 309 of the Companies Code or under Section 33 of the Securities Industry Code that the Company was under an obligation to pay at the date of liquidation; but this is a qualified priority - if ordinary unsecured creditors have been paid at the time of the order, that prior distribution is not to be upset (see Section 442). Note - these orders relate to investigation expenses incurred by the Commissioner for Corporate Affairs.

(xiii) Ordinary unsecured creditors, both national and international.

(xiv) Deferred creditors - consisting of unsecured claims for interest in excess of 12% per annum before liquidation, claims for interest bearing debts after liquidation, claims by joint creditors of a partnership of which the liquidated Company was a member, and debts due to members in their capacity as members.

(xv)   Any surplus is to be paid to the beneficial shareholders in accordance with their rights and interests in the Company.

Creditors secured by a floating charge over the assets of the Company, as distinct from those who hold a fixed charge, must rank after employee entitlements and certain debts to the Commissioner of Taxation, should there be insufficient assets available for payment of these claims. Section 446 of the Companies Code provides that those employee creditors claiming priority for wages, leave of absence, or retrenchment pay must be paid in priority to the claims of the secured creditor and may be made out of the property comprised in or subject to that charge. The same priority is afforded to unremitted group (PAYE) tax, prescribed payments tax, and withholding tax deductions by the Income Tax Assessment Act. For these purposes, as much of the assets subject to the charge as are needed to satisfy these particular claims become available to the Company.

To the extent to which the security is insufficient to discharge the secured creditors' claim (whether the charge be a fixed or floating charge), the balance ranks for a dividend with the unsecured claims. Funds remaining after the payment of priority creditors and secured creditors are available for distribution to unsecured creditors.

(B) CREDITORS' CLAIMS AND PAYMENT OF DIVIDENDS

Procedures exist for the Liquidator to call for proofs of debt and other information to enable him to:

• Assess the rights of creditors to vote at meetings; and

• Admit a creditor for dividend purposes.

There is provision for adjudication, rejection, appeal, and for notifying creditors of, and advertising potential dividends. Claims may also be amended. Having invited proofs, it may be necessary to deal with them within a certain period.

Formal proofs need not be invited unless there is some prospect of a dividend. A Liquidator may instead invite informal claims from creditors. To invite formal proofs where there is no potential dividend would unnecessarily require the submission of detailed proof from creditors without justification in terms of likely compensation.

Creditors prove their debt by submitting certain documentation to the Liquidator who deals with it and determines whether those claims will be admitted to rank for a dividend in the winding up.

A claim is provable if it falls within the terms of Section 82 of the Bankruptcy Act, which provides that all debts and liabilities:

• Present or future,

• Certain or contingent,

• To which the Company was subject at the date of liquidation, or

• To which the Company may become subject after the date of liquidation by reason of an obligation incurred prior to liquidation

are provable.

The Liquidator will distribute funds to creditors whenever he is in a position to do so. However, before distributing, he needs to settle a list of creditors by adjudicating to the fullest possible extent on creditors' claims and by providing for those creditors where his adjudication has not been finalized. The distribution must be preceded by a Notice of Intention to Declare a Dividend to creditors who have not proven and by a Notice in the Commonwealth Government Gazette.

3.2.7 Creditors' Rights to Information — Part of the Liquidator's responsibility is to report to creditors on the conduct of the administration, including the method and results of realizing the Company's assets, the circumstances leading to the winding up of the Company and the results of any investigations.

The two major methods of report are the written reports mailed to creditors and verbal reports given to meetings of creditors. Usually both will be used, with the written report being dispatched for consideration by creditors prior to meetings, allowing them to decide whether it is appropriate for them to attend such meetings. As a matter of practice, meetings are not well attended, particularly in smaller liquidations.

The Liquidator's initial communication with creditors may simply be to advise them of his appointment and call for proofs of debt. However, in his first formal written report, the Liquidator will need to comment on assets available, his strategy of realization for the assets and on his success in carrying it out. The report as to affairs document should also be summarized and the actual realizations compared with the estimated values shown for the assets in that report, together with a summarized statement of the Liquidator's receipts and payments.

If possible, the report should attempt to give creditors an indication of the likely dividend ultimately payable to creditors after allowing for the ranking of priority creditors and the costs of liquidation.

When the Liquidator has completed an investigation of the insolvent Company's affairs, the results of that investigation, so far as they can be included without prejudicing any future litigation, should be incorporated in a written report to creditors.

3.2.8 Termination of Proceedings — A voluntary liquidation might be invalidated by a prior application to the Court for a Court winding up, or a Court order, though this is rare. The liquidation may be terminated by an order for a stay of winding up, if, for example, a scheme of arrangement is proposed and accepted.

When the affairs of the Company are fully wound up, the Liquidator must convene a final meeting of the Company and its creditors. One month's notice by post and in the Commonwealth Government Gazette is required and the Liquidator must lodge his final account of receipts and payments at the Corporate Affairs Commission within one month after the meeting and a Return Relating to Final Meeting within one week after the meeting. No quorum is necessary at the meeting.

The Company is automatically dissolved three months after filing with the Commission a return of that meeting.

A Liquidator must retain the books and records of the Company for a period of five years unless consent is obtained from the Committee of Inspection or creditors generally and the Corporate Affairs Commission.

3.3 Court Liquidation — Court Liquidation, also known as Official Liquidation, provides an opportunity to force the winding up of a corporation against the wishes of corporate management or ownership. This facility is particularly helpful to creditors and oppressed minority members.

Court liquidation is not necessarily involuntary. A corporation may seek its own Court winding up as an alternative to the nonjudicial procedure of voluntary winding up, particularly if there is some urgency to freeze the Company's position.

Court liquidation is a statute-defined procedure permitting the winding up of a

Company's affairs by application to the Court and the orderly distribution of assets among creditors and, if surplus is available, members.

A major benefit to creditors of a Court liquidation compared with a voluntary liquidation is the comfort that the Liquidator has had no previous association with the debtor Company and that he is completely independent. Although, in reality, a Liquidator nominated by the members of a debtor Company is also a professional accountant required to fulfil his responsibilities and act independently, creditors frequently view any preference by members with suspicion.

Court liquidation also allows creditors an avenue to pursue their claims to the point where the debtor Company is compulsorily wound up. This may be a creditor's only alternative when the debtor Company does not voluntarily initiate a winding up.

The major differences between Court liquidation and voluntary liquidation are as follows:

- The Liquidation is commenced by filing an application with the Court which ultimately leads to a judicial order. In a voluntary liquidation, a special resolution of members initiates proceedings.
- The Liquidator is an Official Liquidator, an officer of the Court who conducts the administration on behalf of the Court. In a voluntary liquidation, the liquidator is only required to be a registered Liquidator, who becomes an officer of the Company.
- The proceedings leading to the appointment of a Liquidator are judicial.
- A creditor, a member, the Commission, or the Company may initiate a Court winding up.
- The Court has discretion to order a winding up. Liquidation is automatic in a voluntary winding up if procedure is correctly followed.
- Some cause or circumstance why the Company should be wound up must be proved. No such requirement exists in voluntary proceedings.
- Assuming a winding-up order is ultimately made, the winding up may be immediately commenced by the filing of an application. A voluntary winding up does not commence until the passing of the special resolution at a general meeting, which may require up to three weeks' notice.
- The (Official) Liquidator is chosen by the Court. In some states, an applicant can nominate a Liquidator; however, in New South Wales the appointment is on an automatic rotation basis. In a creditors' voluntary liquidation, members choose a Liquidator although creditors have the opportunity to replace him at the creditors' meeting.
- No meetings are mandatory. In voluntary windings up, annual meetings and a final meeting are required by the Companies Code.

- The Official Liquidator requires permission from either the Court, the Committee of Inspection, or creditors generally to carry on business for the beneficial disposal of assets after the expiration of four weeks from the date of liquidation. Alternately, in a voluntary winding up, the Liquidator does not require permission to carry on business for the beneficial disposal of assets.

3.3.1 Commencement of Proceedings

(a) Winding-Up Application

A creditor may file an application (petition) with the Court seeking an Order to wind up a Company. The Company, a member, the Corporate Affairs Commission, an Official Manager, or a voluntary liquidator may also apply to the Court for a winding-up order. An application to the Court by such parties is termed a 'Petition.'

There is no restriction on the amount of a creditor's debt before a creditor's petition can be heard by the Court. However, it must be just and equitable that the debtor Company be wound up, and the Court must decide that the Company cannot pay its debts before a winding-up order will be granted.

A Court liquidation is usually initiated by a creditor application, and the most common circumstance leading to an application is the failure of a debtor Company to comply with a demand notice issued by a creditor requiring payment within three weeks after the service of the notice.

The most common circumstances for a Company to initiate an application for a winding-up order are the inability to repay debts, and member/management disagreement.

A winding-up application is a means by which a qualified person files application to the Court for winding up and serves a notice on the debtor Company that he is so applying. There must be statutory grounds for the winding-up application--inability to pay debts is the most common ground. Section 364 of the Companies Code contains the usual grounds for a winding-up order. However, other grounds are available under Section 320 of the Code in the case of oppressive or unjust management, and under Section 352 of the Code where an official management is terminated.

An application is first filed and, after a lapse of time, heard. If at the hearing the application is successful, the Court will make a winding-up order against the Company. Such an order may be made, at the Court's discretion, if a qualified applicant:

- Has evidence of grounds for a winding-up order against the Company;
- Files an application with the Court, and serves it on the Company; and
- The application is ultimately heard by the Court.

(b) Provisional Liquidation

Provisional liquidation is a procedure taken as an interim exercise to allow control over the affairs of a Company during the time between the filing of a petition to wind up the Company and the hearing of that petition. This is usually a period of three to four weeks but can vary according to circumstances. For instance, the hearing of the petition may be deferred for a further period to allow the Company time to propose a scheme of arrangement. The Company, a creditor, or a contributory might seek the appointment and will be required to show that assets are in danger of dissipation, deterioration, or are otherwise in jeopardy and need immediate protection. There will have to be some demonstration of urgency for the Court to agree to the appointment.

Provisional liquidation allows interim control over the affairs of a corporation, and it protects the interests of financial participants in a corporation until such time as an application for winding up is determined. A Provisional Liquidator may also be appointed after a winding-up order has been made if there is an appeal against the order and the decision on the appeal has not yet been made.

The Provisional Liquidator's powers are similar to those of a Liquidator, except as restricted by statutory provision, Court order and the knowledge that a winding-up order may eventually be refused. He has the power to administer Company affairs, but is unlikely to be given the power to realize assets initially, except in the ordinary course of business, or to pay dividends. However, he may seek to wind up some of the Company's affairs if it is in the interests of financial participants to do so.

The Provisional Liquidator may also undertake an investigation into the affairs of the Company to inform the Court of the Company's position at the relevant hearing.

The duties to be performed by the Provisional Liquidator will be set out in the Order of the Court appointing him and it is important that the Provisional Liquidator is fully aware of, and understands the terms of, that appointment. If it is at all possible the terms of the appointment should be discussed with the solicitors seeking the appointment prior to the making of the Order. In this way it is possible to have included in the Order any special terms that may be required. This is only possible, of course, if the Provisional Liquidator has been advised of his pending appointment and has been given some of the facts relating to it. Unfortunately, this often is not the way things happen and in many cases the Provisional Liquidator's first contact with the Company is after the Order is made. Consequently it may be necessary to go back to the Court for further directions if it is found that the Order is not clear or does not cover a particular circumstance.

Unless there are some unusual circumstances, the powers of a Provisional Liquidator are limited to the protection of the assets of the business, or part of it, as a going concern and he will have no power to sell assets or make any distribution of Company property. It may be found during the course of the provisional liquidation that it would be in the best interests of the Company and its creditors for certain assets to be sold (e.g., wasting assets) and the Provisional Liquidator should seek the permission of the Court to do this if it is not already in the Order. It may be in the order through the direction to "carry on the business" if the sale of such asset would be made in the ordinary course of business.

In short, a Provisional Liquidator's powers include taking possession of Company assets, controlling its affairs until the winding-up application is decided, and preserving the Company's assets until they become available to a Liquidator or other administrator or are ultimately returned to the control of directors.

A Provisional Liquidator is appointed by the Court. He must be an 'Official Liquidator,' that is, a person who is registered as a Liquidator and who has additionally been registered as an Official Liquidator with the consent of the Court.

Provisional Liquidation is an 'interim administration' (although it may last for some time), which precedes either of the following:

- A Court liquidation;
- An alternative administration, such as a scheme of arrangement, which may be proposed to resolve the Company's affairs, or
- The withdrawal or dismissal of a winding-up application.

The major advantages of provisional liquidation in comparison to other insolvency administrations include the following:

- Speed of appointment;
- Independent control by an Official Liquidator;
- There is an automatic stay of proceedings against the Company; and
- It empowers investigation to recommend future courses of action.

(c) Court Hearing and Winding-Up Order

At the hearing of a winding-up application, it is common for the debtor Company to fail to appear, resulting in the granting of a winding-up order and the appointment of a Liquidator. At the hearing, the Court may either:

- Grant a winding-up order;
- Dismiss the winding-up application (with or without costs);
- Adjourn the hearing conditionally or unconditionally; or
- Make any interim or other order that it thinks fit.

Uncontested applications are usually heard on affidavit evidence. If the Company appears, then it must give notice of its appearance, witnesses may be cross-examined, and opponents to any evidence by affidavit may be required to appear.

The most common defences, especially in respect of a creditor's application, are to prove solvency or put forward reasons why the applicant creditor has not been paid. If these defences have a possibility of being unsuccessful, the debtor Company should be prepared to tender and pay the outstanding claim.

However, this action will not guarantee the failure of the application to obtain a winding-up order.

If it can be proven that the Company is able to pay its debts and the grounds for the application are insolvency, the application will not succeed. The onus of proof is on the debtor Company or its representative. The Court will look at cashflow as well as the asset verses liability position in determining solvency.

The Company may have a genuine cross-claim dispute or defence against the applicant creditor. If the Court considers that there has been insufficient opportunity to pursue that defence, it may refuse to make a winding-up order, but if the defence could earlier have been raised in prior proceedings, it will not necessarily prevent a winding-up order being made.

When a winding-up order is made, the corporation enters into liquidation on the date of the order, although the order must be formally entered in compliance with the Court's requirements. The Official Liquidator is notified of his appointment by the Court Registrar. In New South Wales, the Official Liquidator is required to publish notice of his appointment in the Government Gazette and a prescribed newspaper within seven days. In other states the requirement to advertise and gazette is placed upon the applicant or his solicitor.

Where an order for winding up is made or an application withdrawn or dismissed, notice of that fact must be lodged by the applicant with the Corporate Affairs Commission within two business days after the fact.

The applicant must also within seven days after the passing and entering of an order for winding up, file a copy of the order with the Commission, serve a copy on the Company, and deliver a copy to the Liquidator with a statement that the order has been served.

Additionally, the Liquidator must, within 14 days after his appointment, file with the Commission notice of his appointment and address.

3.3.2 Liquidator — In a Court winding up the Liquidator must be an Official Liquidator. An Official Liquidator is an individual (a professional accountant) who is registered as a Liquidator with the Corporate Affairs Commission and is, additionally, registered with the Commission (with the consent of the Court) as an Official Liquidator. His function is to assist the Court in the winding up of Companies. An Official Liquidator must, prior to this appointment, consent in writing to be appointed, whether as a Liquidator or a Provisional Liquidator.

The procedure for selecting or advocating the appointment of a particular official liquidator and for securing his written consent is at the discretion of the Court of each particular state, which lays down Court rules for the procedure.

Except in South Australia, the A.C.T., and New South Wales, the applicant must, before the hearing of his application, apply to a designated Court officer to have that Court officer nominate in writing the official Liquidator who is to be appointed if a winding-up order is to be made. In Victoria, the officer is the Protonotary; in other States, the Court Registrar.

The applicant then obtains and files the consent of the Liquidator.

Although both the original nomination and the actual appointment stem from the Court, in practice the applicant often suggests the nominee, and the applicant's suggested nominee is often appointed Liquidator.

In the A.C.T., the applicant secures and files the consent of an Official Liquidator at the time of the application.

In South Australia, the applicant merely files the consent of an Official Liquidator to act within 14 days of the issue of the summons for a winding-up order. Effectively, this becomes the Court's nomination.

However, the Court has discretion to select a Liquidator of its choice on making the order, and the practice differs between the States.

In Queensland, for example, the applicant's nominee is usually chosen; whereas in Victoria, a roster system operates which permits the applicant to suggest a nominee.

In New South Wales there is an 'A' list and a 'B' list of Official Liquidators. Those on the 'A' list are deemed to have automatically consented to any appointment and are bound to accept any appointment as Liquidator by the Court. Those on the 'B' list may be appointed in cases in which they consent. Generally, in windings up by the Court, Liquidators are usually appointed in rotation from the 'A' list. 'A' list Liquidators have wide experience in windings up by the Court, and the Court tends to favor appointing persons from this list. However, the Court has a discretion and may be persuaded by evidence of special circumstance to appoint a Registered Liquidator who is not on the 'A' list.

The policy of rotation eliminates favoritism and maintains independence.

The duties of a Liquidator in a Court winding up are similar to those of a Liquidator in a creditors' voluntary liquidation, except that he is an Officer of the Court and not the Company, and is subject to the additional restrictions imposed by the Court and other legal constraints.

For example, a Court Liquidator requires the consent or authority of either the Court, a meeting of creditors, or the Committee of Inspection to carry on business for the beneficial disposal or winding up of that business for longer than four weeks, whereas a Liquidator in a voluntary administration does not have such a requirement.

3.3.3 Report as to Affairs — A report as to the Company's affairs (a statement of assets and liabilities) is required to be prepared by the Directors and Secretary of the Company and submitted to the Liquidator. In practice the Liquidator usually assists in this exercise.

The Liquidator may also serve a notice in writing on other persons connected with the Company requiring them to submit reports containing information specified in the Liquidator's notice regarding the affairs of the Company.

The report required from the Directors and Secretary must be submitted automatically within 14 days after the liquidation date. Where information is requested from other persons associated with the Company, they are required to submit it within 14 days after receiving the notice requiring them to do so. Procedures are available for the granting of extensions of time.

The report as to affairs document acts as an aid to the Liquidator and it provides a guide to creditors or members as to the Company's estimated financial position at the time of the liquidation.

A summary of the report is usually sent by the Liquidator to creditors and contributories prior to the convening of an initial meeting.

After receiving any reports, the Liquidator must file copies with both the Court and the Corporate Affairs Commission within seven days of receipt.

He is also required to lodge a copy of any notice of extension of time granted by him with the Commission.

When the Liquidator is unable to obtain a report as to affairs, because of non-cooperation by Company officers, because he is unable to locate them, or for any other reason, he should report that fact to both the Commission and the Court.

3.3.4 Committee of Inspection — In a compulsory Liquidation, the Committee of Inspection has the same composition and role as in a Creditors' Voluntary Liquidation. The Committee is similarly appointed by, and acts as representative of, creditors and contributories. In this regard, readers are referred to paragraph 3.2.5 for further detail.

3.3.5 Assets Available to Creditors — Any property that belonged to the Company at the commencement of the winding up or that was acquired by the Company after the commencement of winding up, is available to the Liquidator for the benefit of creditors. The Liquidator is empowered to take into his custody or under his control any property to which the Company is or appears to be entitled.

Any disposition of Company property after the commencement date other than by the Liquidator or by Court Order is void unless validated by the Court.

Therefore, property available is that which belonged to the Company at the commencement of the winding up, or has been acquired by the Company after the commencement of winding up.

Property available is not limited to that property which was under the control of the Company at the date or occurrence of the liquidation. A Court liquidation commences at the time of filing the application for winding up, unless the Company had previously commenced to be wound up voluntarily.

In a voluntary winding up, "commencement" and "date" of liquidation are the same date.

In the case of a Court winding up, the commencement date is to be compared with the date of liquidation, being the date on which the Court makes and enters a winding-up order. While the date of liquidation is the date when legal disabilities descend on the Company, the effect of an earlier deemed commencement, when combined with other provisions of the Code, is to make some legal disabilities retrospective.

The retrospective period between the date of the liquidation and the commencement of liquidation is referred to as the "relation back period."

Any property owned by the Company at the deemed commencement, or acquired by it after that date, which has been disposed of by the date of liquidation, is recoverable by the Liquidator under a qualified doctrine of relation back. This does not apply to exempt property and the Court may validate certain dispositions or classes of disposition, thereby protecting assets from recovery.

In addition to available property, certain property may be recoverable by the Liquidator or certain obligations declared void by virtue of separate statutory provisions.

Voidable transactions may occur before or after the commencement of liquidation, however recovery is not possible for exempt property and protection is afforded to certain types of transactions. Exempt property includes property held in trust for another person, and the proceeds of insurance against liabilities to third parties. In circumstances in which the person who has dealt with or acquired the property in question has acted in good faith, for valuable consideration, and in the ordinary course of business, the transactions are usually protected.

Subject to particular exemptions, protective provisions, and to the rights of special creditors, the property that a Liquidator may have available for distribution or may recover is summarized as follows:

- Property owned by the Company at the date of liquidation;
- Property owned by the Company at the date of the filing of the application for winding up, but disposed of before the date of liquidation, which is available under a qualified doctrine of relation back. Similarly, property acquired by a Company after the date of the filing of an application for winding up but disposed of before the date of liquidation.
- Property or income acquired or earned by the Company after the date of liquidation.
- The proceeds of certain executions and other related legal proceedings in the possession of a third party.

- Property disposed of by the Company in a settlement or transfer that occurred within the five years preceding the commencement of the liquidation (voidable settlements).

- Property that was disposed of by the Company with an intent to defraud creditors (fraudulent dispositions).

- Property or consideration transferred to a creditor within, or after, a period of six months before the filing of an application for winding up, or voluntary resolution with the effect of giving the creditor a preference over other creditors (voidable preferences).

- Where a disposition confers a preference upon a creditor and at the same time has the effect of discharging an officer of the Company from a liability, whether contingent or otherwise, the amount of that benefit (indirect preferences).

- Damages recoverable from directors or officers of the corporation in consequence of their breach of common law duties to the Company and its financial participants.

- Moneys recoverable from Directors, managers, and other persons in consequence of personal liability being imposed on them for obligations incurred by the Company that amount to reckless or fraudulent trading.

- Undue profits made on sales to/purchases from the corporation by directors, promoters, and related persons, when such sales/purchases are made within the four years before the commencement of the winding up.

- Property charged by way of floating charge to a secured creditor, where the charge was created within six months of the commencement of the winding up, and is invalidated for lack of new consideration.

- Property charged to a related person, when he has attempted to enforce the charge within six months of its creation without Court permission.

- Property charged to any secured creditor when the registration of such a charge is required under the Code, and the failure to comply makes the charge invalid against the Liquidator.

3.3.6 Creditors' Position — Creditor remedies against a debtor Company are restricted by liquidation, with a right of claiming by proof of debt against the Company generally replacing the right to continue pursuit of action against the Company. However, winding up does not deny secured creditors their rights under their securities. The ordinary remedies of which a creditor is deprived include proceeding to judgment and levying execution on a judgment. The intention is to replace these and other remedies with equitable distribution under winding up.

(a) Priority of Claims

The same priorities for the ranking of creditors' claims in a creditors' voluntary liquidation are applicable in a Court liquidation. The only difference being that the taxed costs of the winding-up applicant are regarded as an additional cost of the winding up, which ranks equally with the Liquidator's remuneration and expenses. In this regard, the reader is referred to paragraph 3.2.6 A.

(b) Creditor Claims

As with a Creditors' Voluntary Liquidation, the same procedures exist for the Liquidator to call for proof of debt claims from creditors in respect to their outstanding debts at the date of liquidation (the date of the winding-up order).

Only a provable debt that has been admitted by the Liquidator can rank for repayment in the form of a dividend distribution. A notice of dividend is sufficient notification of the admission of a debt or claim. The liquidator does have power to admit a debt or claim without formal proof; however, he cannot reject a debt or claim without first requiring the submission of a formal proof of debt claim.

If there appear to be insufficient funds available for a distribution to certain classes of creditors, then the Liquidator will usually not call for proofs of debt from these creditors.

The amount provable by a creditor, including interest where chargeable, is to be computed up to the date of the winding-up order, unless a voluntary winding up had previously commenced.

A creditor must state on the proof of debt whether he is a secured creditor, together with the value and nature of his security (if any) and whether the debt is secured wholly or in part. When inviting proofs of debt, a Liquidator will set a time for their lodgment, and when inviting them in connection with the payment of a dividend, he is required to set specific times.

(c) Dealing with Proof of Debt Claims

The Liquidator must determine which creditors have just and legal debts so that he can distribute the surplus assets of the administration among these creditors. He should not admit any claim that appears doubtful, and he must require sufficient evidence to dispel that doubt.

The Liquidator must examine:

- The nature of the debt to see whether it is provable or is in fact excluded from that category;
- Any set-off claimed to determine whether the creditor is so entitled;
- Whether the creditor is of a class entitled to any priority of repayment or, conversely, to deferred repayment;
- The validity of any security claimed by the creditor, including its proper registration;
- Where the creditor claims to be entitled to interest, the justification for this, and the method of calculation; and
- The evidence provided by the creditor comparing the amount claimed with

the amount shown in the Company's report as to affairs and if necessary with other records of the Company.

He may have to seek further information or evidence from the creditor or from the Company.

At the end of this process, he will then be in a position to decide whether to admit or reject the proofs of debt.

(d) Dividends to Creditors

The Liquidator should declare a dividend to admitted creditors as soon as practicable, and he should distribute all moneys in hand subject to retention of funds to cover the costs of the liquidation. Even if all assets have not been realized, the Liquidator should still declare an interim dividend if sufficient funds are on hand. However, prior to any distribution to unsecured creditors, priority creditors must be paid or provided for, and unproved unsecured creditors must be given the opportunity to prove their claims.

A creditor has no recourse against a Liquidator for a dividend; however, if the Liquidator has sufficient funds after paying an interim dividend and subsequent to the dividend he receives an additional proof of debt claim, he is obliged to pay a dividend on that claim. In the instance in which a Liquidator is negligent or refuses to pay a dividend, a creditor may apply to the Court for an order for the Liquidator to pay a dividend.

When a dividend is declared, notice must be given in advance to all creditors whose debt or claim has not been admitted, providing them with the opportunity to prove prior to the dividend declaration.

The following procedure should be employed by a Liquidator when inviting proof of debt claims from creditors:

- A date should be fixed for creditors to prove their claims by--this date should be not less than 14 days from the date of the notice inviting creditors to prove.
- A notice must be sent to all known creditors who have not already proved.
- An advertisement calling for proofs should be placed in a daily newspaper.

Before distributing a dividend, the Liquidator must advertise his intention to do so in the Commonwealth Government Gazette. This notice must be published not more than two months prior to the intended date of the dividend.

The Liquidator must also notify in writing known creditors who have not as yet been admitted of his intention to declare a dividend. This notice must specify a date by which a proof must be admitted to participate in the distribution and this date must be at least 21 days after the date of the notice. Creditors who do not submit a proof by that date are excluded from participation in that dividend. A dividend may be declared immediately after the expiration of the period in which proofs must be lodged.

In Western Australia and Tasmania, a certified list of proofs received in a Court liquidation and the actual proofs admitted or rejected are required by Court Rules to be filed monthly with the Court.

When the dividend is declared, the Liquidator must send notice of the declaration accompanying the payment to each creditor receiving a dividend. A person entitled to receive a dividend may lodge an authority with the Liquidator directing the Liquidator to pay the dividend to another person, in which case the Liquidator is to comply with that direction.

A Liquidator in a Court winding up has the same responsibilities in reporting to creditors as does the Liquidator in a creditors' voluntary winding up.

3.3.7 Termination of Proceedings — Upon finalization of the Company's affairs, the Liquidator may apply to the Court for dissolution of the Company. He would only make such application when the winding up has been completed and if there are sufficient assets to fund a Court dissolution. He may simultaneously apply for his release as Liquidator; however, his application for release is not mandatory and is often neglected in practice.

The dissolution application requires the preparation of an affidavit bringing to the Court's attention relevant matters concerning the conduct of the administration and the attitude of the Commissioner for Corporate Affairs to the conclusion of the administration.

Should there be insufficient assets in a Court liquidation, an application is made to the Commission to have the Company struck off the register. Such an application does not involve a release of the Liquidator. Unless consent is obtained from both the Court and the Commission, the Liquidator must retain the Company's books and records for at least five years.

B. Partnerships, Joint Debtors, and Individuals

3.4 Bankruptcy — Bankruptcy is the only form of terminal procedure available in Australia for partnerships, joint debtors, and individuals (noncorporate debtors).

Bankruptcy may be instigated through the Court by a Creditor (involuntary Bankruptcy) or voluntarily by the debtor himself filing a petition with the Registrar in Bankruptcy. Either an insolvency practitioner (a registered trustee) or the Official Trustee (a Government body) may act as Trustee for the purpose of investigating and administering the debtor's affairs, realizing assets, and paying dividends. The laws and requirements of bankruptcy are contained in the Commonwealth Bankruptcy Act 1966, as amended, and Statutory Rules made under that Act.

A bankruptcy occurs when a sequestration order is made by the Court (upon application/petition of a creditor) against the estate of a debtor or, alternatively, when the debtor's own petition to become a bankrupt is accepted by the Registrar in Bankruptcy.

A debtor may be made bankrupt more than once, and whether or not he is still undischarged from an existing bankruptcy. A debtor may also be made 'bankrupt' after his death by an order for an administration of his deceased estate.

As an alternative to bankruptcy, a debtor may enter into a Part X Arrangement, or informal arrangement, with his creditors as detailed in paragraphs 2.4 - 2.8.

3.4.1 Commencement of Proceedings

(i)   Involuntary Bankruptcy

A creditor may present a petition to the Court against a debtor, or against partners or joint debtors, seeking a sequestration order against the debtor's estate. The debtor must have committed an act of bankruptcy and have certain connections with Australia.

A creditor's petition can be presented by a creditor alone or jointly with others, if:

- He is owed at least $1,000 by the debtor;

- The debt is a liquidated sum, payable either immediately or at a certain future date; and

- An act of bankruptcy has been committed by the debtor within the six months before the presentation of the petition

There are a number of potential acts of bankruptcy. The most common alleged is the failure of the debtor to comply with a formal bankruptcy notice requiring payment of the debt within a fixed period. A creditor must obtain a judgment or similar Court order in respect of the debt before he can issue a bankruptcy notice.

The Court has a discretion whether to make a sequestration order on a creditor's petition, and will not exercise that discretion if it regards the debtor as able to pay his debts, or for some other reason considers that making the order would be inequitable.

If a sequestration order is made against the debtor's estate, the debtor becomes a bankrupt.

(ii) Voluntary Bankruptcy

A debtor may become bankrupt voluntarily, by filing his own petition. A debtor's petition is one presented by a debtor against himself and includes a petition presented against a partnership and presented by joint debtors against themselves. The debtor becomes bankrupt if and when the petition is accepted by the Registrar.

There is no monetary limit specified for a self-petition, and the debtor (except in the case of partnerships) need not have any residence in or business connection with Australia, in contrast to the requirements of a sequestration order. Nor is there any requirement that the debtor be unable to pay his debts, although this is likely.

A debtor's petition may be presented against a partnership by a majority of partners resident in Australia at the time of presentation. When there are joint debtors who are not in partnership with each other, any two or more of such debtors may present a petition jointly against themselves.

The Registrar will automatically accept an individual debtor's petition provided it is in acceptable form. The same applies to joint debtors. However, in the case of a partnership, unless all the partners have petitioned, the Registrar may refer the petition to the Court to enable the Court to exercise its discretion as to the acceptance, amendment, or rejection of the petition.

3.4.2 Appointment of a Trustee — A sequestration order will not be made, nor a debtor's petition accepted, unless:

- A registered trustee has consented to act; or
- If he has not consented to act -

    (i) the debtor's property is less than $10,000, or

    (ii) the petitioner has taken all reasonable steps to obtain, but has been unsuccessful in obtaining, the consent of a registered trustee.

In the absence of a consent when the debtor is made bankrupt, the Official Trustee will act as the trustee in bankruptcy. Hence, with the exception of small bankruptcies, a registered trustee must be sought by the person initiating the bankruptcy. The Registrar in each bankruptcy district has a list of registered trustees that he will make available to intending petitioners.

Most registered trustees are accountants in private practice, usually belonging to one of the professional bodies, such as the Institute of Chartered Accountants in Australia or the Australian Society of Accountants.

3.4.3 Information for Creditors — A trustee has the power to convene first and subsequent meetings of creditors. A first meeting is not mandatory unless the trustee is requested by a creditor to convene it. However, a trustee will summon a meeting whenever he wishes to report to creditors first hand, to consult with them formally, or to appoint a committee of inspection of creditors' representatives to assist him.

A registered trustee will also need to convene a creditor or committee meeting to secure approval for his remuneration. The various meeting requirements for notification, advertising, rules of conduct, voting restrictions, and proxy usage are contained in the Act and Rules. Briefly, the notice of meeting to be mailed to creditors must provide seven days' clear notice of the meeting date. If it is a First Meeting, the meeting must be advertised in the Commonwealth Government Gazette, and in such other newspapers as are considered appropriate by the Trustee. Advertising is not mandatory for meetings other than the First. The notice should contain an agenda, a summary of affairs, a proxy form, and a proof of debt form. A trustee's report to creditors, while not mandatory, should also accompany the notice of meeting to provide creditors with material to consider prior to the meeting.

The bankrupt must attend a First Meeting of Creditors and, if required by the trustee, attend subsequent meetings.

Whether there be meetings of creditors or a committee or not, the trustee should attempt to report in writing to creditors regarding:

- The bankrupt's property and likely dividend to creditors;
- The conduct of the trustee's administration; and
- The circumstances leading to the bankruptcy of the debtor and his conduct, dealings, and transactions.

3.4.4 Assets Available to Creditors — The property available to the trustee for the benefit of creditors is generally that which belonged to the bankrupt at the commencement of the bankruptcy (prior to the actual date of bankruptcy), or is acquired by him after commencement but before the bankrupt's discharge from bankruptcy. The Bankruptcy Act grants various exemptions to specific property of the bankrupt being claimed by the Trustee, such as:

— Ordinary tools of trade, plant and equipment, professional instruments, and reference books to a total value of $2,000;

— Necessary wearing apparel;

— Necessary household property;

— Certain insurance policies and proceeds arising from policies in force for periods of between two and five years;

— Certain rights to personal damages or compensation for the bankrupt or his family;

— Property held in trust for another person; and

— Property whose title has not passed to the debtor.

Property devolving on the debtor after the date of bankruptcy but before discharge is available to the trustee.

The bankrupt is entitled to retain income earned after the date of bankruptcy for his own benefit. It is possible for the trustee to apply to the Court to have some portion of the bankrupt's income paid over for the benefit of creditors generally. The application would only be made and the Court would only make such an order if the bankrupt's income were surplus to his needs. Alternatively, a bankrupt may voluntarily make available after-acquired income for the benefit of creditors.

Once a bankruptcy occurs, it is deemed by law to have commenced at the time of the earliest act of bankruptcy by the debtor within a period of six months preceding the debtor's or creditor's petition. Any property of the bankrupt owned by him at the date of deemed commencement or acquired after that date but not owned at the date of bankruptcy is potentially recoverable by the trustee (the principle of 'relation back'). However, certain defences to recovery are available to the person in possession of the asset or those who received the benefit of repayment, the most common of which are that they dealt with the debtor or a third party in good faith in the ordinary course of business and without notice of the debtor's impending bankruptcy.

Other payments or dispositions that may be recoverable by a trustee include those:

- Undertaken fraudulently,
- Conferring a preference on particular creditors,
- Representing settlements designed to retain benefits for the debtor, or
- Contravening the intention of the Bankruptcy Act to treat creditors equally.

These voidable transactions may occur before or after the commencement of bankruptcy.

3.4.5 Creditors' Position

(i)   Priority of Claims

The general rule of distribution is that all property that belongs to the bankrupt is to be applied in satisfaction of his liabilities equally, but this general rule is subject to many exceptions both within the priorities conferred by the Bankruptcy Act and by other legislation such as the Income Tax Assessment Act, and by commercial practice. For example, the existence of particular security over specified assets; the need to pay a debt to obtain a financial advantage for the estate; or approval by creditors or the Court to specific variations in priorities.

Property legally secured or charged to a particular creditor, while technically divisible among creditors and vesting in the trustee for that purpose, is only divisible subject to the legal rights of secured creditors. The trustee can only inherit the same rights in respect of such property as the debtor had at the commencement of bankruptcy.

The trustee has the right to sell 'secured property;' however, he is required to repay the secured creditor the net proceeds of sale or the amount necessary to discharge the secured creditor in full if that amount is less than the net proceeds of sale.

If there is a deficiency from the sale of the 'secured asset,' then the secured creditor may prove as an unsecured creditor in the Estate for that amount. If there is a surplus, this is available to the trustee for distribution.

The secured creditor retains the right to realize or otherwise to deal with his security.

The priority of distributions in bankruptcy are similar to those in compulsory liquidation. The priority for distribution of available assets to the various classes of creditors, both pre- and postbankruptcy, is specified in the Bankruptcy Act. Subject to certain assumptions and exceptions, the order of priority is as follows:

- Expenses incurred by the trustee (or by his authority) in protecting the assets or carrying on the bankrupt's business in accordance with the Act;
- Fees, percentages, and charges, payable to the Registrar in the bankruptcy;
- Other fees, costs, charges and expenses payable by the trustee in the bankruptcy;
- Repayment of any unused deposit lodged by a petitioning creditor in connection with the appointment of an interim trustee;
- The taxed costs of the petitioning creditor or applicant for sequestration;
- The remuneration of the trustee;
- The reasonable out-of-pocket expenses incurred by a member of the committee of inspection as allowed by the Court;
- The costs of any audit carried out under Section 175 of the Act not being an audit carried out by the Auditor-General;
- Unremitted employee PAYE deductions or withholding tax deductions or prescribed payment tax deductions under the Income Tax Assessment Act (Section 221P, 221YHJ, 221YU) and on unremitted natural resource and royalty payment deductions under Section 221YHZD;
- In the case of a bankrupt who has previously signed an authority under Section 188 (Part X), the remuneration of the controlling trustee and expenses properly and reasonably incurred by him during the period in which the authority is in force, including any debts incurred by the controlling trustee that are provable in the bankruptcy; if the Section 188 authority was given to a solicitor, for taxed costs due to the solicitor in respect of services rendered by him in relation to the authority;
- Where the bankruptcy occurs within two months after a Part X arrangement, or a scheme of arrangement has been declared to be void or been annulled, set aside, or terminated - payment of the liabilities, commitments, expenses, or remuneration of a trustee due under those arrangements;
- If the estate is being administered under the deceased debtor provisions (Part XI), funeral and testamentary expenses therein;
- Amounts due to employees, not exceeding $2,000 per employee, in respect of services rendered to and for the bankrupt prior to the bankruptcy (being salaries, wages, or commission);
- Amounts due in respect of compensation payable under any law of the Commonwealth or of a State or Territory relating to workers' compensation, being compensation the liability for which accrued before the date of the bankruptcy. This priority does not apply to the extent to which the bankrupt

is indemnified under a contract of insurance against that liability; and it does not apply to the amount payable by a bankrupt by way of reimbursing the funds under any law of the Commonwealth, etc., that provides for workers' compensation. When the compensation payable under a law is payable by way of periodical payments, a lump sum for which those periodical payments could, if redeemable, be redeemed under the law, is the relevant amount;

- Amounts due to or in respect of any employee of the bankrupt for long service leave, extended leave, annual leave, recreational leave, or sick leave for the period before the date of bankruptcy;
- Apprentice indenture fees overpaid;
- Preferences, priorities, advantages, costs, charges, or expenses that a meeting of creditors, by special resolution and with special notice, agrees to;
- Ordinary unsecured creditors;
- Deferred creditors; and
- Any surplus, after payment of all categories above, to the bankrupt.

Statutory subrogation is provided to those who have paid employees' wages or leave, which if unpaid would rank in priority. The persons who have paid may rank for priority repayment.

Exceptions occur if the Court orders priority of the repayment to be given to creditors who provide financial support for the recovery, preservation, or realization of assets, and when creditors agree by special resolution to give priority to a creditor, cost, charge, expense, or class of creditor (as indicated in the above list).

(ii) Creditor Claims and Repayment of Dividends

Creditors prove their debts by submitting certain documentation, including a Proof of Debt form, to the trustee who determines whether he shall admit those claims to rank against the estate.

A claim is provable in a bankruptcy if it falls within the terms of Section 82 of the Act which provides that all debts and liabilities:

- Present and future,
- Certain or contingent,
- To which a bankrupt was subject at the date of bankruptcy, or
- To which he may become subject before his discharge by reason of an obligation incurred before the date of bankruptcy, are provable in his bankruptcy.

A trustee of a bankrupt estate must declare and distribute dividends with all convenient speed among the creditors who have proved their debts, subject to the retention of sufficient funds to meet the costs of administration or to give effect to the provisions of the Act.

Subject to providing for these costs, all moneys in hand are to be distributed. Although all assets may not have been realized, interim dividends should be declared and paid. Before any dividend can be declared in favor of unsecured creditors, the position of priority creditors must be allowed for; so, too, must the position of any unsecured creditors of which the trustee is aware who have had insufficient time to prove their claims.

When all funds are realized or as much is realized as can be without needlessly protracting the bankruptcy, the trustee must declare and distribute the final dividend, specifically calculated without regard to debts not proved at the time of declaration.

No action lies against the trustee for a dividend. If the trustee is negligent or refuses to pay a dividend, a creditor may apply to the Court to have the Court order a trustee to pay a dividend. In such a case, the trustee may be required personally to pay interest on the dividend without recourse to the estate.

Although creditors may furnish an authority in writing to the trustee for him to pay someone else on their behalf, only those creditors whose proofs have been admitted are to rank for dividend.

In the calculation and distribution of the dividend, a trustee will allow sufficient time for communication difficulties and must allow for debts provable that, despite having been lodged, have not yet been admitted.

When a dividend is to be declared, notice must be given in advance to all creditors who have not proved their debts, providing them with the opportunity to prove before the dividend is declared.

The bankrupt is entitled to any surplus remaining after payment in full of the costs of the administration of the bankruptcy, all debts proved in the bankruptcy and interest on interest-bearing debts proved in the bankruptcy.

3.4.6 Investigation and Examination — The trustee has a responsibility to ascertain the assets and liabilities of the bankrupt, and, if he considers it appropriate to do so, to investigate the conduct, dealings, and transactions of the bankrupt, the cause of bankruptcy, and his books and records. Such an investigation would concern itself with any unusual events, offences or transactions that may give rise to potential claims or asset recoveries.

The trustee may also elect to have the bankrupt publicly examined on oath as to his conduct, trade dealings, property, and affairs. This examination may be used to seek evidence in relation to a potential recovery or litigation. The trustee, or a creditor, may examine the bankrupt and the transcript of the examination may be used in evidence in proceedings against the bankrupt.

Persons other than the bankrupt may also be examined if they might be indebted to or have property of the bankrupt, or otherwise be capable of giving information about the bankrupt's affairs.

3.4.7 Finalization of the Bankrupt Estate — A bankrupt is discharged automatically upon the expiration of three years from the date of the bankruptcy, unless an objection is made by the Registrar, the trustee, or a creditor, and the objection is upheld. Alternatively, an order for discharge may be sought by the bankrupt by application to the Court prior to the expiration of this three-year period.

The effect of a discharge of the bankrupt is to release him from all provable debts, although he continues to have a duty to assist the trustee in the realization and distribution of the estate.

The Court also has power to annul the bankruptcy if, for example, it is satisfied that the sequestration order ought not to have been made or that the debts of the bankrupt have been paid in full.

A deed or composition by the bankrupt with his creditors may be accepted by the Court after bankruptcy and, if so, the bankruptcy may, subject to the discretion of the Court, be annulled.

The trustee of a bankrupt estate may either apply for release on the conclusion of the administration or, alternatively, will be automatically released upon expiration of seven years from his furnishing of a final account in respect of the bankrupt estate.

The books and records of the bankrupt, which he is required to submit to the trustee during the course of the bankruptcy, will then, in practice, be returnable to the bankrupt unless he instructs the trustee to destroy them.

The trustee may destroy his own administrative records only with the written permission of the Registrar, or 25 years after his appointment.

4. TYPES OF SECURITY AND ENFORCEMENT

Security can be created by contract, such as a mortgage, pledge, or charge, or arise by operation of law, such as a lien.

Most charges, whether legal or equitable, created by a company over its assets must be recorded in the company's file at the Corporate Affairs Office in the State of incorporation of the company.

It is important to note that, for the most part, it is the individual States and Territories that govern the question of security and enforcement and, in some cases, such legislation differs. Consequently, professional advice should be sought in the relevant region.

4.1 Land and Buildings

An interest in land can be "freehold," effectively meaning complete and unqualified, or "leasehold" where rights depend on the payment of a rent for a limited period of years (with or without a capital payment for the grant of the lease).

(a) Torrens Title System

By far the vast majority of land is registered under this system and the title, as registered, to such land is guaranteed by the State.

Land so registered bears a series of identification numbers to specify its location. All charges (i.e., mortgages), given they are in the required form, are noted on the title once registered.

Consequently, interest in property must be registered at the Titles Office in the relevant State to give effective security. Any number of successive charges or mortgages can be granted on a property. Traditionally, the mortgage creates an obligation on the mortgagor to maintain the property to a given standard.

The title to the land can be transferred without the consent of the mortgagee; however, his security over the property remains intact.

(b) Other Systems

Specific legal advice should be obtained when dealing with land controlled other than by the Torrens Title System.

The general law or Old System Title operated whereby legal ownership is conveyed to the mortgagee contrasts with the Torrens Title System where a statutory charge is created in favor of the mortgagee with title continuing to vest with the existing owner (mortgagor).

An "Equitable Mortgage" (an informal but nevertheless effective arrangement) is normally organized by depositing the title deeds with the lender, but there must be the intention to create a mortgage; the mere possession of the deeds is not sufficient evidence of a charge over the property.

Obtaining, registering, and enforcing security over leasehold property, while possible in respect of Torrens Title System property and other land, differs significantly between the individual States and depending on how the land is registered.

4.2 Ships

Special rules apply to ships, and the rights of creditors can vary markedly from that established in relation to other assets. It is essential that specialist advice be obtained when considering the effect of maritime nonstatutory liens and other charges.

Mortgages of ships fall outside the scope of some otherwise relevant legislation (e.g., Bills of Sale Acts).

4.3 Livestock and Crops

Special rules apply in relation to livestock and crops.

The Bills of Sale Acts apply in some cases; however, as different rules apply in different States and some States do not apply tests consistently to all species, it is important to seek specific advice.

Generally, effective security can be obtained over the income and the capital (i.e., the apple and the tree, the wool and the sheep).

4.4 Other Assets

Other tangible assets may be given as security by either mortgage or pledge.

Where the debtor remains in possession of the goods, the various Bills of Sale Acts prima facie apply. Various requirements regarding registration and terms, in particular the right to seize property,must be complied with for a Bill of Sale to be effective. Once again there is considerable inconsistency between the various States and Territories although basically once registered the creditor can seize and sell the property subject to the security if payment or performance by the debtor is unsatisfactory. Sufficient proceeds from the sale can be retained to satisfy the debt.

Hire purchase arrangements in which the debtor does not obtain legal title to the goods, although he does enjoy possession until the complete purchase price is paid, are a means of security commonly used in the sale of household effects.

A creditor may be able to effect payment by enforcing a lien. There is a wide variety of liens that can be claimed in different circumstances.

Solicitors' and bankers' liens, where certain documents or funds may be withheld until payment is received for services rendered, are examples of effective Common Law liens as is a repairer's refusal to release your vehicle until they have been paid.

In certain circumstances a subcontractor can claim an effective lien over monies due to the principal contractor pursuant to the Subcontractors Charges Act. This is an example of a Statutory lien. The Crown is entitled to the benefits of a Statutory lien in some cases.

Although less common, intangible assets such as insurance policies, patents, copyrights, goodwill, or partnership shares may also be used as security.

Paragraph 4.7, "debentures," looks at a common means of obtaining security over tangible and intangible assets.

4.5 Retention of Title

It is becoming increasingly common for suppliers to attempt to retain title to goods supplied until they have received full payment.

The retention of title clause must form part of the original contract for supply and not merely appear on the invoice and, depending on the wording of the clause, the contract can amount to a form of security that requires to be registered. This involves practical difficulties and, although retention of title can be effective, recent case law has tended to restrict the occasions on which title can in practice be retained by a supplier.

4.6 Personal Security

Personal guarantees are frequently required from directors or major shareholders of a company, particularly by bankers and major suppliers when the debtor company has not been trading for long or has a very low paid-up capital.

It is often advisable for personal guarantees to be supported by formal security over the guarantor's assets such as their residential dwelling.

4.7 Debentures

A debenture is an acknowledgment of indebtedness. It may be either a single debenture in favor of one lender (usually the company's banker) or a series of debentures or debenture stock, which may be bought and sold in the same way as company shares. A debenture does not automatically grant security, although most debentures (strictly termed mortgage debentures or secured debentures) are worded so that they do, in fact, secure the indebtedness concerned.

Where a series of debentures is issued, it is common for an institution to be appointed as trustee on behalf of the individual holders. The trustee can exercise all the powers of the debenture holders so that his position is similar to that of a single holder. Debentures are widely used to secure overdrafts and loans from companies' bankers and other financers.

(a) Form of Debentures.

The debenture is a written document usually sealed (officially signed) by the company creating it, containing an undertaking by that company to repay the sums due on a specified date or on demand.

It also includes the details of interest rate applying to the outstanding loan along with a schedule of the types of assets over which the debenture gives security. The rights of the mortgagee to appoint a Receiver or to enter into possession themselves is also spelled out.

(b) Property Covered by Debentures.

A company may charge any of its assets, including uncalled capital, goodwill, and future assets. The security given will either be a fixed charge or a floating charge.

A fixed charge is a mortgage of specific assets and this is normally restricted to property such as land, book debts, and goodwill.

A floating charge is a form of security that is said to 'float' over various categories of assets, such as machinery, equipment, or inventories, but it is not fixed because the company is allowed to deal with the assets concerned (for example, by converting its raw material stocks into finished products for sale or to dispose of machinery due for renewal) without the problems of disposing of mortgaged assets; new or replacement assets obtained automatically become the subject of the floating charge.

The holder of such a debenture is, therefore, able to maintain a charge over all the assets of the company (which are not already encumbered) while allowing the company to trade in the normal way.

If a receiver is appointed under the terms of a floating charge debenture (or on liquidation, or on the occurrence of any event specified in the debenture deed), the floating charge 'crystallizes,' that is, becomes a fixed charge, and all the individual assets covered by the floating charge form part of the security of the debenture-holder. The operation of a floating charge is sometimes difficult for other creditors to understand, especially if goods they have recently supplied are deemed to form part of the security of the debenture-holder, although the suppliers themselves remain unpaid.

5. DEBT COLLECTION PROCEDURES

5.1 Commercial Practice

To achieve optimum realization of debts due, prompt action is required in documentation and follow up of outstanding debts. Procedures that can be effective include the mailing of pressing requests for payment, and follow up of the debtor by telephone demands. The procedure available under the Companies Code to apply to the Supreme Court for a winding-up order against a corporate debtor can be effectively utilized in pressing for payment of debts due.

When internal collection procedures have not resulted in payment, debts should be placed in the hands of solicitors or debt collection agencies to follow up on a timely basis and, when economically viable, to implement legal action to enforce collection.

5.2 Legal Proceedings

Procedures involved in the collection of debts include:

(a) Judgments: Proceedings against a debtor may be initiated by a "writ" or a "summons" from a court of appropriate jurisdiction - this will depend upon the size of the debt. For smaller debts, the use of a default summons may enable the entry of a judgment in the event of the debtor failing to notify of his intention to defend the proceedings within a prescribed time - usually 21 days.

(b) Writs of Execution: In the event of a debtor failing to pay on a judgment, the creditor may apply to the Court for a Writ of Execution that authorizes the Sheriff or Bailiff to seize and realize a debtor's property for the benefit of the creditor. Such action may be stopped if the debtor goes into liquidation or is made bankrupt. Further, if such occurs soon after the satisfaction of the debt, a liquidator or trustee may be able to declare the payment void as an undue preference and compel repayment to the estate.

(c) <u>Garnishee Orders</u>: On occasions, Courts may on application, issue orders to garnish bank balances, book debts, and wages of a debtor such that they are directed toward satisfaction of the creditor's judgment debt.

(d) <u>Charging Order</u>: A creditor may be able to obtain a charging order (i.e., a mortgage or charge created by the Court) over certain assets of a debtor to the extent to which they are not already mortgaged.

(e) <u>Order for Liquidation/Bankruptcy</u>: For Corporate debtors, a creditor may petition the Court for the winding up of the Company when a demand for payment remains unsatisfied for 21 days. The creditor need not have a judgment to make such a demand. The threat of such proceedings is often a strong weapon in pursuing payment of a corporate debt.

For Individuals and Partnerships, a creditor must first obtain a judgment before proceeding. Application may then be made to a Registrar in Bankruptcy for the issue of a Bankruptcy Notice. Failure by the debtor to pay within the prescribed time (usually within 21 days of being served with a Bankruptcy Notice) is deemed to be an "act of Bankruptcy," and entitles the creditor to issue a petition to the Court for a Sequestration Order (i.e., the compulsory bankruptcy of the debtor). This procedure is also a powerful weapon for inducing debt payment; however, as it requires first a judgment, it is generally a slower procedure than in the case of companies.

6. SOURCES OF LAW

6.1 Statutory Law

Company law in Australia is administered by the States rather than by one Federal Act. The basis of the legislation is derived from English Law, however, until 1961 minor variations occurred between the six State Acts and the Ordinances of the Territories. In 1961, the States agreed to enact uniform companies legislation (Uniform Companies Act 1961) to facilitate matters for companies dealing in more than one jurisdiction. After several minor amending Acts, the legislation was more comprehensively revised by the Companies Act, 1981, enacted by the Federal Parliament, and contemporaneously by each of the six States - referred to as the Companies (Name of State) Code (e.g., Companies (New South Wales) Code). Each Code is supported by Companies Regulations, which detail certain of the procedures set out in the body of the legislation. Further procedures are specified by Supreme Court Rules in each jurisdiction.

The insolvency laws relating to unincorporated partnerships, sole traders and individuals are contained in the Bankruptcy Act, 1966 (as amended). Unlike company law, the bankruptcy of natural persons is administered by one Federal Act.

Certain provisions relating to the adjustment of creditors' claims and the avoidance of undue preferences are imported from the Bankruptcy Act, 1966, into the Companies legislation by Sections 431 and 451.

The priority of the Crown for certain classes of federal taxation is given force by the Income Tax Assessment Act, 1936 (Sections 221P, 221YU, and 221YHJ) and the Crown Debts Priority Act, 1981. Other legislation that may, on occasion, override the provisions of either the Companies Code or the Bankruptcy Act include the Defence Service Homes Act,   ; the Family Law Act, 1975; and various State Acts relating to Employment and Labor.

6.2 Case Law

In addition to statute law, many fundamental principles of company and insolvency law are based on cases decided in the civil courts. Case law is bound by the principle of legal precedence, and decisions generally follow those of equivalent or higher Courts within the Commonwealth of Australia, or on occasion, by reference to cases decided in other Commonwealth countries, such as England, Canada, and New Zealand.

The major Courts of jurisdiction for Companies are the State Supreme Courts; and for individual Bankruptcies, the Federal Court.

7. SOURCES OF INFORMATION

7.1 Registries

In each State there is a Corporate Affairs Commission.

Members of the public may inspect companies' files during normal business hours and obtain microfiche copies of the information recorded therein for a small fee.

The information kept on a company's file includes:

a. copies of its constitution documents (memorandum and articles of association);

b. names, addresses, and other particulars of its directors and secretary;

c. the address of its registered office (i.e., its legal address);

d. details of all mortgages and charges over its assets; and

e. annual return forms, containing lists of shareholders and details of the company's financial affairs.

In each State there is a Registrar in Bankruptcy and the public may search the records kept there during normal business hours for a nominal fee.

In each State there is a Land Titles Office that records real estate, and mortgages thereon.

7.2 Publications

Formal notices in winding-up and bankruptcy proceedings must be published in the Commonwealth Government Gazette or a State Government Gazette, and some notices must also be placed in local newspapers.

Credit reference agencies publish regular lists of judgment orders made against businesses, and details of appointments of receivers and liquidators.

7.3 Other Sources of Information

Banks may reply to requests for information on the standing of their customers, provided that the request is made in writing, and relates to specific and genuine transactions. Legal responsibility for such information is disclaimed.

All letterheads of every company must disclose the company's name and its place of incorporation. Any company carrying on a business under a name that is not its own must disclose the company's own name on all business documents and at each place of business.

CANADA

Canada
Table of Contents

CANADA

NOTES ON LEGAL SYSTEMS AND PROCEDURES IN CANADA

Canada has courts of both provincial and federal jurisdiction, a result of powers shared by the provincial and federal government pursuant to the Constitution Acts 1867 and 1987. Section 91 of the Act sets out 29 specific areas of federal jurisdiction, including:

— Regulation of Trade and Commerce
— Raising of Money by Taxation
— Banking
— Bankruptcy and Insolvency

All the provinces and territories follow the English common law except Quebec, where the law is based on the Civil Code. Each province's superior court has the inherent jurisdiction to try virtually all cases in which a wrong has been committed. The superior courts of each province or territory are:

Prince Edward Island (P.E.I.)   — Supreme Court of P.E.I.

Nova Scotia   — Supreme Court of Nova Scotia

New Brunswick   — Court of Queen's Bench

Newfoundland   — Supreme Court of Newfoundland

Quebec   — Superior Court of Quebec

Ontario   — Supreme Court of Ontario

Manitoba   — Court of Queen's Bench

Saskatchewan   — Court of Queen's Bench

Alberta   — Court of Queen's Bench

British Columbia   — Supreme Court of British Columbia

Northwest Territories   — Supreme Court of Northwest Territories

Yukon   — Supreme Court of Yukon Territory

The Supreme Court of Canada is an appellate court of civil and criminal jurisdiction. Decisions of each province's or territory's Court of Appeal may be appealed to the Supreme Court of Canada (with the leave or permission of the Supreme Court of Canada).

INSOLVENCY PRACTITIONERS

The Bankruptcy Act provides for the appointment of a licensed Trustee to administer the affairs of insolvent companies or persons who file an Assignment in Bankruptcy or proposal pursuant to that Act. A person is licensed by the Minister of Consumer and Corporate Affairs after having obtained membership in the Canadian Insolvency Association (a three-year program) and such further examination and investigation as the Minister deems appropriate. Licensed Trustees tend to be accountants. There is also provision for corporate Trustees, which tend to be corporations affiliated with the major accounting firms. There are certain requirements for bonding of Trustees by the Minister and there are also specific bonding requirements associated with each estate administered by the Trustee. To file an Assignment in Bankruptcy in Canada it is necessary for the corporation or person first to find a Trustee willing to act. If they are incapable of finding a Trustee willing to act, the Official Receiver, who is appointed by the Superintendent of Bankruptcy who is appointed by the Minister of Consumer and Corporate Affairs, will appoint a person in that locality to act.

There is no licensing requirement for receivership, agency, liquidation, winding-up, or other appointments. Generally an accountant is used; however, there are no prerequisites and no licensing requirements.

The Canadian Insolvency Association was formed in 1982 in an attempt to establish a professional body capable of self-regulation with rules and standards of professional practice. Presently, the Canadian Insolvency Association is introducing professional guidelines and standards that will be applicable to their members. However, there are many licensed Trustees who are not affiliated in any fashion with the Canadian Insolvency Association.

1. TYPES OF BUSINESS ENTITIES

While there is little restriction on the legal form that a business may adopt, the principal form of entity is the limited company (limited, ltd., incorporated, inc.). Partnerships and sole proprietorships are predominately encountered in smaller enterprises. Limited partnerships are unusual, and tend to be found in real estate or resource development situations.

1.1 Limited Companies

There is no distinction between privately-held and publicly-traded limited companies. However, to obtain a listing on a stock exchange, the company must meet certain criteria established for publicly-traded entities. These are not important to this guide as they have no effect on the primary responsibility for paying creditors' claims.

A limited company is a legal entity, distinct from its shareholders, that provides those shareholders with limited liability in the event of the company's insolvency. The company may own property and sue and be sued in its own name.

The company is bound by its articles of incorporation. These articles define the company's objectives, constitution, and internal regulations (which are usually set out in the form of bylaws). All limited companies must have either the word "Limited" or "Incorporated" as part of their name (often abbreviated to Ltd. or Inc.).

The company's operations are directed by its officers, who are responsible to the company's directors; these officers do not need to be directors of the corporation. There is no requirement to have the employees' interest represented on the Board of Directors. Although there are no requirements in terms of numbers of officers or directors, at least one director must be appointed to be responsible for the company. While the corporation's shareholders, officers, and directors have limited liability from the company's creditors, there are instances in which the company's officers and directors can be found liable for certain of the company's indebtedness.

Companies may be incorporated under either federal or provincial jurisdiction. Ordinarily a company intending on operating nationally would incorporate under the federal statute, and one intending on operating in one province would incorporate under the appropriate provincial statute. However, there is provision for a provincially incorporated company to commence operations in another province by obtaining a license to operate in that jurisdiction.

There are requirements for filing annual information returns. These filings, which are available to the public, include information about the nature of operations, number of shareholders, and the company's directors and officers.

1.2 Partnerships

Partnerships are most commonly:

(a) Professional practices, whose professional rules do not allow the members' liability to be limited; or

(b) Small concerns with a set number of principals that do not require the protection of limited liability.

It is necessary to register partnerships involved in trading, manufacturing, and mining. While there is no statutory requirement to register the operating name of partnerships involved in other types of operations, it may affect their right to sue or be sued and is considered prudent business practice.

Each partner is jointly and severally liable for all the partnership's debts and obligations.

While there is no restriction on the maximum number of partners in a partnership, there must be a minimum of two. Ordinarily, dealings between the partners are documented in the form of a partnership agreement drafted at the partnership's initiation. There is no legal requirement for such an agreement, but it does assist in a more orderly wind up of operations in cases of partnership break-up.

1.3 Limited Partnerships

To a lesser extent than ordinary partnerships, limited partnerships have been utilized in Canada in some cases for developing real estate or natural resources. The limited partnership consists of any number of limited partners who have a financial interest only; the project is supervised by one or more general partners.

Limited partnerships must be registered with the appropriate provincial body. General partners have unlimited liability, whereas the limited partners' liability is limited to the extent of their original investment. Where limited partners are found to have become directly involved in the partnership's operations, they may be construed to be general partners without limited liability.

1.4 Sole Proprietorship

Individuals who carry on a business and own its operations are referred to as sole proprietors. While not required legally, a sole proprietor commonly registers his or her operating name with the appropriate provincial body. Sole proprietors may not trade in a name or style identical to other business entities and, accordingly, they usually perform a search prior to utilizing a particular name. There are no requirements to file any financial or other information with any government body.

1.5 Other Entities

Other entities within Canada include:
- Registered Charities
- Registered Nonprofit Associations
- Crown Corporations
- Banks, Insurance Companies, and Trust Companies
- Joint Ventures

Registered charities and nonprofit associations must be registered and approved by the federal government, which provides for their tax-exempt status and allows them to receive donations that are tax deductible by the donors. These entities are not specifically precluded from insolvency proceedings. When they are limited companies, liability may be attached to the directors in their personal capacity for certain statutory or other trust claims.

Crown corporations are corporations specifically provided for in an act of a provincial or federal parliament. Examples of crown corporations are:
- Air Canada
- Canadian National Railways

- Federal Business Development Bank

Banks, insurance companies, and Trustee companies are specifically precluded from filing for bankruptcy under the Federal Bankruptcy Act. In recent years, there have been several cases in which Canadian regulatory agencies have found such entities to be insolvent. Such cases require use of the Winding-Up Act for trust companies and insurance companies, and the specific winding-up provisions of the Bank Act for chartered banks.

2. REORGANIZATION PROCEDURES

Little legislation in Canada provides for reorganizing business entities. If a company is insolvent (i.e., its assets are less than its liabilities) and has no trust deed debt outstanding, the only formal means for it to negotiate a settlement with its unsecured creditors is legislated under part 3 of the federal Bankruptcy Act. The rights of secured creditors cannot be affected under the Bankruptcy Act. The only legislation under which the claims of secured creditors can be compromised is the Companies' Creditors Arrangement Act (C.C.A.A.) and then only if the company has trust deed debt outstanding. Accordingly, it is not uncommon for companies to resort to informal compromise or be placed in receivership by their secured creditors.

There is no distinction between the various business entities discussed previously and their rights or entitlements to relief through any of the reorganization procedures noted below.

2.1 Informal Compromise

Many companies or other business entities that have a severe cash flow shortage or that are in an insolvent situation will resort to informal compromise in an attempt to continue uninterrupted operations. The informal compromise has no legal basis other than the contractual arrangement negotiated between the company and its creditors.

By entering into an informal compromise, the corporation admits its insolvency to its creditors, and therefore subjects itself to potential formal bankruptcy proceedings. It is also subject to action from any creditor who refuses to accept the informal compromise. Accordingly, unless the company's proposal is accepted by 100 percent of its creditors, an informal compromise will not ensure its continued viability.

2.2 Proposal Under Part 3 of the Bankruptcy Act

In Part 3 of the Bankruptcy Act, provision is made for a company or individual to make a proposal to its creditors. Such a proposal maybe made by anyone who is either insolvent (as defined under the Act) or who is bankrupt.

The proposal must be supervised by a Trustee licensed by the government to administer bankrupt estates. It may take any form providing for an extension of time, repayment scheme, or other financial arrangement with the creditors.

The debtor files information with the Trustee with respect to the proposal and his assets and liabilities. The Trustee examines the debtor's affairs, which he, the Trustee, reports at the meeting of creditors held to consider the proposal. This meeting, held on a minimum of 10 days' notice to the creditors, results in a vote by them. The proposal is considered accepted if creditors holding 75 percent of the value of the outstanding claims vote in favor of it.

If accepted, the Court reviews the proposal and either gives it final approval or rejects it. If the proposal is rejected by either the creditors or the Court, the debtor is automatically bankrupt.

Filing the proposal effects a stay of proceedings on all creditors except those with security over the debtor's assets.

The proposal's filing does not result in any of the debtor's assets being vested in the Trustee named in the proposal. Accordingly, the advantage of a proposal is that it effects a stay of proceedings against the ordinary creditors while not taking away the debtor's control of its operations or assets. To offset this, of course, the debtor's activities will have to be established as forthright because all interested parties, including the Court, will scrutinize the proposal and its terms, the debtor's activities, and the benefits to the creditors versus a bankruptcy. Because rejection results in automatic bankruptcy, a proposal presents a great risk for the debtor. Also, the debtor must ensure that he has the total and complete cooperation and endorsement of all secured creditors because the rights to repossession bestowed on secured creditors are outside the Bankruptcy Act.

2.3 C.C.A.A.

The C.C.A.A. does not apply unless the debtor company has outstanding an issue of secured or unsecured bonds, debentures,debenture stocks, or other evidences of indebtedness issued under a trust deed or other instrument running in favor of a Trustee; and the scheme of compromise or arrangement that is proposed must involve a compromise or arrangement between the debtor company and the holders of such an issue. The C.C.A.A. is ordinarily used where a large company is insolvent and it is necessary to make an arrangement with shareholders, debenture holders, and unsecured creditors. If the rights of shareholders are to be affected, the arrangement will proceed under the C.C.A.A. in coordination with appropriate federal or provincial corporate legislation. An application is made to a superior court judge and an order obtained directing the holding of meetings of the various classes of persons affected by the arrangement. If the application is accepted by the creditors, a further application is made to the court for approval. If approved, it becomes binding on both assenting and dissenting creditors.

2.4 Receivership

Receivership is not ordinarily considered a reorganization procedure in Canada; it is usually instituted against the debtor's wishes.

Receivership can result in paying the secured and unsecured creditors' claims and restoring the company to profitable operations. However, more frequently the company is sold as a going concern or ceased and the assets liquidated. Receivership is a procedure available to a creditor with security over some or all of the debtor's assets. It is designed principally to protect the security interest of the creditor for whose benefit the receiver is appointed.

The secured creditor must first have valid security against some or all of the company's assets. Second, the security document must provide for appointing a Receiver and/or Receiver/Manager. Although the Receiver has only those rights which are set out in the security document, the document usually includes a provision for his right to manage the company's operations if all the corporation's assets are encumbered.

Appointing a Receiver by a secured party requires demand of the indebtedness and sufficient notice to the debtor of its intention.The adequacy of the notice period is the subject of several important legal decisions. The notice requirement and the debtor's general reluctance to admit a Receiver has, in some instances,resulted in secured lenders applying to the court for a Receiver/Manager's appointment. Such an appointment generally prevents the unsecured and preferred creditors from enforcing judgments or other claims against the assets secured by the security documents.

The Receiver has certain duties and obligations to the debtor. The courts have determined that the Receiver acts in a dual capacity as the secured creditor's agent as well as the debtor's agent.

2.4.1 Appointment of a Receiver — While anyone may be appointed a Receiver (there are no professional requirements or qualifications), secured lenders usually seek professional accountants who have some insolvency experience. Except for a Court appointment, the debtor generally has no input in selecting the Receiver. However, in some circumstances the debtor's cooperation is obtained through negotiation.

The Receiver usually obtains independent legal counsel and seeks an opinion on the security under which he was appointed to ensure its validity and to identify other secured parties who may be in priority to his position.

A Receiver/Manager may also be appointed under a Court order. Such an appointment may be obtained under various circumstances including:

(1) Shareholder/Partnership disputes.

(2) Matrimonial disputes.

(3) Where a secured creditor is unable to obtain the debtor's cooperation and consent.

In cases of Court appointments, the Court hears applications from all interested parties regarding whom to appoint as Receiver or Receiver/Manager.

2.4.2 Receiver's Powers — A privately-appointed Receiver's powers are determined by the document under which he has been appointed. These powers ordinarily include the right to take possession of, and realize on, the assets charged by the security under which he has been appointed. Typically, security documents containing floating charge provisions provide for the Receiver to manage and to realize on the debtor's assets as he sees fit. Generally, a Receiver will realize a greater amount for the debtor as a going concern rather than a break-up liquidation value for the assets. Therefore, it is not unusual for the Receiver and Manager to continue the debtor's operations for a short period to determine its viability and the possibility of a going concern sale.

Occasionally, in receiverships of corporations, the Receiver will transfer certain assets into a newly incorporated subsidiary company for a price that is established only when the subsidiary's shares have been sold. This procedure was adopted from the United Kingdom process known as "hiving down." This process does not affect the rights of the debtor's creditors.

Any purchaser of assets from a Receiver is under no obligation to the creditors of the company in receivership.

In cases of Court appointments, the Receiver obtains his authority and powers directly from the Court, acts as an officer of that Court, and is responsible to no other party. The Receiver requires court approval for all his actions and may frequently have to reattend to obtain either changes to the original Order or additional provisions to enable him to carry out various activities.

2.4.3 Receiver's Obligations — The Receiver's overriding obligation is to act honestly and in good faith and to deal, in a commercially reasonable manner, with the assets covered by the security under which he has been appointed.

The Receiver may also have some general obligations under various provincial corporate statutes. While such legislation varies across Canada (some provinces have no provisions relating to Receivers), a Receiver in private appointments is generally considered obligated to take possession and control of the assets secured, maintain a separate bank account, account for all transactions entered into,and to report to the appointing party periodically and on completion.

While the Receiver is not specifically obligated to report on his activities to unsecured or preferred creditors, a corporation's officers or directors, and other interested parties, he is an agent of the debtor and not just of the secured creditor. Accordingly, in practice, the Receiver will communicate with the creditors at the start of his appointment to notify them of the receivership. However, he will rarely provide any detailed information after that time.

The Receiver is not obligated to pay outstanding debts at the time of his appointment except those secured on assets in priority to the security under which he was appointed or which specifically have priority according to statute. Those statutory obligations have resulted in many very highly publicized legal actions in Canada. The jurisprudence indicates that several federal and provincial bodies have either statutory liens or "deemed trusts" in priority to any form of security on the debtor's assets. Anyone involved in a receivership must be aware of the potential for these claims and their priority. (These are not detailed here due to changes in jurisprudence and statutory legislation.)

The Receiver is liable for all obligations that the debtor incurs after his appointment.

The Receiver's remuneration is approved by the secured creditor or the Court but is generally paid out of the debtor's assets in receivership.

2.4.4 Termination of the Receivership — A court-appointed Receiver is obligated to fulfill all duties and obligations set out in the Court Order as issued or subsequently amended. Upon completing these duties and obligations, the Receiver will report to the Court and have his accounts passed; at that time the Court will discharge the Receiver.

There is generally no set procedure for discharging a privately appointed Receiver. He may issue a final report to the secured lender or request an indemnification from the secured party.

A contentious issue in private appointments occurs when funds are realized above and beyond the secured party's indebtedness. There is little jurisprudence covering how the Receiver may dispose of such funds. Generally, it is considered most appropriate to turn them over to the corporation's officers and/or directors. Ordinarily, the Receiver will circulate a letter to the creditors advising them of his intention to do so on a specific date. This allows the creditors an opportunity to pursue any rights or remedies and make any arrangements they wish.

2.5 Orderly Payment of Debt

Under Part 10 of the Bankruptcy Act, individuals not conducting business for themselves may apply to the Court for an Order consolidating all debts and settling for monthly payments to allow them to repay all creditors' claims in full. While this procedure is provided under a federal statute, the statute's provisions are administered by the provinces. (It is available in all provinces except New Brunswick, Newfoundland, Ontario, and Quebec.)

Although procedures may differ between provinces, the debtor contributes amounts earned over and above his reasonable personal expenses to the administrator on a monthly basis. The administrator will then obtain the creditors' approval to this arrangement.

All debts must be paid within three years or the debtor must obtain an extension from Court. While the consolidation order is in effect there is a stay of proceeding against all creditors.

3. TERMINAL PROCEDURES

3.1 Bankruptcy

Bankruptcy is legislated under a federal Act which applies to limited companies and individuals. It excludes building societies having a capital stock, incorporated banks, savings banks, insurance companies, trust companies, loan companies, and railway companies.

The proceedings may be commenced voluntarily (the debtor makes an assignment under the Act) or involuntarily (a creditor petitions the court for the debtor's bankruptcy; or on the refusal by the creditors or the court of a proposal made by the debtor).

In the petitioning process, the creditor must have a claim of at least $1,000 and be able to prove an act of bankruptcy by the debtor. Acts of bankruptcy are defined in the Bankruptcy Act. The most commonly used definition is if the debtor "ceases to meet his liabilities generally as they become due." With a minimum of eight days' notice to the debtor, the Court will hear both parties' evidence, and if it adjudges the debtor bankrupt, will issue a Receiving Order effectively placing the debtor in bankruptcy.

In Canada, the parties involved in bankruptcy proceedings include:

(a) Trustee — a person licensed by the federal Minister of Consumer and Corporate Affairs to administer bankrupt estates, generally accountants.

(b) Superintendent of Bankruptcy — a person appointed by the federal government to oversee the conduct of Trustees in all bankruptcy proceedings.

(c) Official Receiver — persons appointed by the Superintendent of Bankruptcy who work for the federal government in all major centers across Canada with whom all bankruptcies must be filed and who receive various reports from the Trustee regarding the administration of the bankrupt estates under their control.

(d) Registrar — a provincially appointed court officer who deals specifically with bankruptcy matters and has powers to hear ex parte applications, and review bills of account and such other matters as are provided under the Bankruptcy Act.

3.1.1 Commencement of Proceedings — To make a voluntary Assignment in Bankruptcy or to have a petition for a Receiving Order heard, a Trustee lieensed by the Superintendent of Bankruptcy must be named. Most major accounting firms have licensed trustees in their offices.

Once the Receiving Order is issued, or the Assignment filed, the debtor provides the Trustee with a statement of affairs. This document summarizes the debtor's assets and liabilities.

The bankrupt (or an officer of the corporation by resolution of the Board of Directors) is responsible for adhering to various duties outlined by the Bankruptcy Act. These include:

(a) delivering all his property to the Trustee;

(b) delivering all books and records to the Trustee;

(c) attending for examination before a representative of the government department in charge of bankruptcy filings;

(d) providing the Trustee with a statement of affairs;

(e) assisting the Trustee in the inventory of his assets;

(f) attending a meeting of his creditors; and

(g) assisting the Trustee in realizing on his property.

All of the bankrupt's property (except certain personal belongings outlined in provincial statutes in cases of assignments filed by individuals) vests in the Trustee immediately upon the issue of a Receiving Order or on the filing of the assignment.

3.1.2 Duties and Obligations of the Trustee — The Trustee is obligated to realize on the debtor's assets and to distribute that realization, after providing for his fees and expenses, to the creditors.

In addition, the Trustee has the right, duty, and/or obligation to:

(a) take possession and make an inventory of all assets;

(b) take possession of the books of account;

(c) take whatever conservation measures are necessary or obtain whatever legal advice is required prior to receiving the creditors' instructions;

(d) carry on the bankrupt's business if he considers it necessary in the interests of the estate;

(e) verify the bankrupt's statement of affairs;

(f) mail notice of the bankruptcy to all creditors within five days of the bankruptcy;

(g) call a meeting of creditors within 19 days of the bankruptcy;

(h) maintain a separate bank account for the realizations in the estate;

(i) ensure that the bankrupt's property is insured;

(j) make whatever statutory reports are necessary on behalf of the bankrupt; and

(k) file with the Court a report on the bankrupt's conduct so the Court may make a decision regarding the bankrupt's discharge.

3.1.3 First Meeting of Creditors — As indicated previously, a first meeting of creditors is held within 19 days of a Receiving Order or of the assignment being filed. This meeting is ordinarily presided over by a representative of the Official Receiver.

The meeting's principal purposes are to:

(a) hear and discuss a report from the Trustee about the bankrupt's activities prior to the assignment, the bankrupt's assets and liabilities and such other matters as the Trustee sees fit;

(b) have the creditors affirm the Trustee's appointment or substitute another Trustee;

(c) have the creditors appoint inspectors to oversee the Trustee's activities and to assist him in his administration; and

(d) provide other direction to the Trustee as the creditors see fit.

Only unsecured claims may be voted; voting is on the basis of the amount of the creditor's claim. Creditors receive one vote for every claim between $25 and $200, an additional vote for claims between $200 and $499, a further additional vote for claims between $500 and $999, and yet another vote for each incremental $1,000 or portion thereof being claimed (i.e., a creditor with a claim of $1,100 would be entitled to four votes).

The inspectors, called for under the Bankruptcy Act, are appointed by the general body of creditors at the first creditors' meeting. There must be between one and five inspectors in any estate. Naturally, they must be independent of any contested action or proceeding by or against the estate and may not acquire any property from the estate.

The Trustee has numerous powers, with the inspectors' approval,but has little capability to act in the estate's administration without the approval of a majority of the inspectors. The inspectors' obligation is to assist the Trustee in administering the estate and to verify the bank balance and Trustee's accounts. Ultimately, they approve the Trustee's final statement of receipts and disbursements. For these functions, the inspectors receive a nominal fee from the estate.

3.1.4 Distributions to Creditors — When notifying the creditors of the bankruptcy, the Trustee also provides them with a proof of claim form, which they complete. If the claim is supported by adequate documentation, the Trustee enters it against the estate. The claims are entered in different rankings, as set out in Section 107 of the Bankruptcy Act, which provides for the priority of distribution to these creditors. This priority ranking is:

(a) administration costs;

(b) a 5 percent levy payable to the Superintendent of Bankruptcy;

(c) employees' wages and expenses to a maximum of $500 each;

(d) municipal taxes;

(e) rent payments to a maximum of three months in arrears and three month accelerated;

(f) various Crown claims; and

(g) all other unsecured claims.

At distribution, assuming there is one, the Trustee pays all claims in each of the above categories in that order. If there is more than one claim in a particular category, and insufficient funds to pay all those claims, the available funds are distributed pari passu.

There is a provision for certain claims to be deferred until all the claims of other creditors have been paid. Such claims include those of related parties for wages and those arising from preferential transactions.

Secured creditors are allowed to file as unsecured for the difference between the amount of their claim and that realized on any assets. Secured creditors may accrue interest on their indebtedness until the date of realization; however, no other claimant is allowed interest after the date of bankruptcy.

3.1.5 Discharge — Ultimately, the bankruptcy process results in a hearing for the bankrupt's discharge. However, this discharge process is applicable only to individuals. The sole circumstance under which corporations may obtain a discharge from bankruptcy is if their creditors are paid 100 cents on the dollar.

The Trustee prepares a report outlining the bankrupt's conduct and whether he has fulfilled his duties as required under the Bankruptcy Act. The Court reviews his report and decides whether to discharge the bankrupt.

Three types of discharge are available:

(1) Absolute discharge — bankrupt is discharged absolutely from all indebtedness at the date of bankruptcy.

(2) Conditional discharge — bankrupt is discharged from all indebtedness at the date of bankruptcy upon fulfilling one or more conditions.

(3) Suspended discharge — bankrupt is discharged from all indebtedness at the date of bankruptcy after a specified period of time expires.

The Trustee may not apply for a bankrupt's discharge until after three months from the date the assignment is filed. During the period that the bankrupt is undischarged, he is obligated to fulfill his duties and to comply with various other obligations including:

(a) having limited use of credit;

(b) disclosing the fact that he is an undischarged bankrupt in any situation in which credit is obtained or in any business transaction; and

(c) being unable to act as a corporation's officer or director.

Information about an individual's bankruptcy is public information for seven years after the date of discharge.

3.1.6 Debts Not Discharged — Certain debts are not discharged by the discharge order whether it is absolute or otherwise. These are set out in Section 148 of the Act and include:

(a) fines or penalties imposed by a court;

(b) debt for alimony, maintenance, or support;

(c) debt arising as a result of fraud or fraudulent misrepresentation;

(d) liability for the dividends any creditor not notified of the bankruptcy would have received had the creditor been aware of the bankruptcy and filed a claim; and

(e) debt or liability for goods supplied as necessities of life.

It is incumbent on the creditor to institute proceedings after the discharge for recovering his debt and proving to the Court that it is covered by Section 148.

3.2 Liquidation

While the Bankruptcy Act applies to most corporations and is by far the most frequently applied when terminating a company's operations, in certain instances it is necessary to implement the liquidation of a corporation. These are strictly court proceedings and involve applications by interested parties for a liquidation order.

The Court appoints a liquidator who acts as an officer of the Court. Although the company's property does not vest in the liquidator, he can carry on the business of the corporation for the purpose of winding up its affairs. He is also responsible for fulfilling the Court Order and for liquidating the company's assets, the proceeds then being distributed to its creditors as ordered by the Court.

3.3 Winding Up

In Canada, the federal Winding-Up Act deals with the winding up of trust companies, insurance companies and railway companies, and certain noncommercial entities.

There are also provisions in federal and provincial corporate statutes permitting the orderly winding up of the affairs of corporations wishing to close operations. These are not, however,directed at insolvency situations.

4. TYPES OF SECURITY AND ENFORCEMENT

In Canada, the law regarding security and enforcement among the various assets to be used as security varies between provinces. There is no uniform code across the country for registering real property and securing an indebtedness against it or within the various categories of corporate assets and personal property both tangible and intangible.

Security in Canada can be created by contract, such as a mortgage, pledge, or charge, or arise by law, such as a lien or attachment order.

4.1 Land and Buildings

At present, there are two systems for registering an interest in land in Canada. They are the Land Titles system and the Land Registration system. All matters involving land and buildings require legal advice; the requirements for registering an interest in, or a security interest against, land or buildings varies between the two systems.

Several successive charges may be granted on a particular property. However, to be valid and in priority to any subsequent charge the mortgage interest must be registered on the property title. Although an unregistered mortgage is still a valid charge, it loses priority over subsequently granted but properly registered charges.

Various government agencies, and more specifically municipalities for land taxes, can create a lien on the land for arrears in priority to any charge thereon. In addition, various provincial utility companies have the right to lien land in priority to mortgage charges previously registered.

In recovering an indebtedness under a mortgage, the mortgagee has the option of either Foreclosure or Power of Sale.

Foreclosure involves a six-month notice period to the owner after which title to, and equity in, the property is vested in the mortgagee. The property owner has the option in the notice period to require that either the property be sold or the mortgage be paid out.

Alternatively, the mortgagee may issue a Power of Sale, a legal proceeding that provides the owner and subsequent encumbrances with 30 days in which to pay out the mortgage. After 30 days, the mortgagee has the right to list the property for sale and convey title to it. Any registration in priority must be paid from the proceeds before paying the mortgagee taking the Power of Sale action.

4.2 Other Tangible Assets

Several provinces provide for registering a security interest in other tangible assets, generally termed the "Personal Property Security System." In those provinces, any interest in the property must be registered under the system if it is to have priority over other security interests.

All security interests must either be in writing or the secured party must possess the goods.

There are innumerable documents that secure assets, including general security agreements, chattel mortgages, conditional sales contracts, assignments of book debts, and assignments of inventory.

Security interests can be granted to secure previously incurred debts, debts incurred at the time the security interest is granted, or future debts. However, when considering an indebtedness' priority, it is most common for the creditor to supply fresh advances sufficient to retire an old indebtedness so that the debt is considered new.

As indicated previously, perfection of the security interest is either by possession or by registration under the personal property security system, if applicable in that province. If by registration, a financing statement must be filed providing a general description of the security involved, the debtor's name, the creditor's name, and applicable agreement and registration dates.

4.3 Retention of Title

To secure their shipments of goods, suppliers must institute a consignment procedure or enter into a purchase money security interest with the debtor. A purchase money security interest must be registered under the personal property security system, if applicable, and all prior secured creditors must be provided with 30 days' notice.

4.4 Personal Security

It is commonplace for banks and others in the financing business to require personal guarantees of directors, principal shareholders, or senior management members. Such a guarantee must be evidenced in writing and signed by the guarantor; registration is unnecessary. In addition, collateral mortgages are commonly obtained by the lending institution against the assets of those guaranteeing the debt. These collateral mortgages are registered against the assets to protect the creditors' potential interest.

4.5 Sale of Encumbered Assets

All security agreements contain a charging clause, and ordinarily contain default clauses which allow the secured party to take possession of the assets if the debtor defaults on repayment. Situations in which an advance was made without a set repayment schedule require a demand prior to repossession. Once the secured party has repossessed the assets, if they were registered pursuant to a personal property security system, a minimum of 15 days notice of the goods' sale must be given to the owner and any other registered secured creditor.

After the notice period expires, the only obligation of the secured party is to dispose of the goods in a commercially reasonable manner.

4.6 Debentures

It is common in Canada to use debentures as a floating charge over a corporation's assets. There are other documents that contain floating charges including most general security agreements.Floating charges are registered under the Corporation Security Registration Act. This system provides for perfection of floating charge security similar to that provided by the provincial personal property security systems. All floating charge security must be registered.

The use of experienced legal counsel is recommended in obtaining or dealing with any security providing a floating charge.

4.7 Bank Act Security

As a specific provision of Section 107 of the federal Bank Act,security is available to chartered banks over various products of the field, forest, and seas; products manufactured from them; and associated equipment. This security interest requires evidencing the debtor's intention to provide the bank with security which is then registered under a federal system to control and regulate this type of security. Again, such security is highly specialized and there are specific provisions for repossessing and selling goods secured in this manner. It is strongly recommended that one use legal counsel experienced in this type of security.

5. DEBT COLLECTION PROCEDURES

Numerous procedures enable creditors to collect debts prior to commencing insolvency proceedings, although some are uneconomical and unwieldy in practice.

5.1 Commercial Practice

Prompt action is essential in collecting debts, and constant reviews of debtors' accounts, followed by regular applications for payment, are necessary. Even when this is done, debtors can easily ignore written reminders for overdue accounts. This is less likely if they are sent by the creditors' solicitors; letters from solicitors or reputable debt collection agencies frequently produce payments.Very often, telephone reminders are more effective in collecting overdue accounts than statements sent by mail; an alternative to the telephone is the telex machine. If the debtor is short of cash, the creditors who exert the greatest pressure are usually the ones paid.

A creditor's ultimate sanction is to threaten to petition the court for a winding-up or bankruptcy order. Notice can be served requiring payment within 14 days, failing which an application will be made to the court for the appropriate proceedings. A court judgment need not be obtained before such a notice is sent. This course carries with it a slight risk that any funds recovered by the creditor after presenting the petition would have to be repaid.

Threatening to commence winding-up proceedings is a powerful weapon,because such a petition (although not a bankruptcy petition) must be advertised, which may adversely affect the debtor's business.Moreover, it is the bank's practice to close the debtor's account once a winding-up petition is advertised. For this reason, winding-up proceedings should not be used for debts that can be collected in other ways.

5.2 Legal Proceedings

Although creditors have the right of personal access to take court action against a debtor, solicitors should be employed to do so. The proceedings will fail if the creditor has not complied with the court's strict requirements. Costs are sometimes awarded to creditors who are successful plaintiffs, but these are determined by the court and are usually not sufficient to pay the solicitors' full fees.

Proceedings available to creditors collecting debts include:

(a) Judgments.

(b) Writs of Execution.

(c) Garnishee Orders.

(d) Equitable Execution.

(a) Judgment

A judgment is obtained by issuing a "statement of claim" and is a Court Order to pay a specific sum of money. Proceedings must be brought in the correct court. Those for claims up to $1,000 (in certain major cities, up to $3,000) can be initiated in small claims courts. Proceedings for claims up to $25,000 should be initiated in district courts, in either the area of the defendant's address or registered office, or in which the contract originated.

If the defendant defaults (i.e., fails to appear and file a defence), an application for summary judgment may be made pursuant to the Rules of Practice.

(b) Writs of Execution

Execution generally refers to enforcing a judgment or court order by an officer of the court, usually the sheriff, taking actual possession of property for the purpose of satisfying the judgment.

If a creditor is unable to obtain payment of a judgment against a debtor who he believes has sufficient tangible assets to pay the debt, he can obtain a "writ of execution" from the court.This is a court order to the sheriff to seize and realize on the debtor's assets.

(c) Garnishing Income and Other Debts

A judgment creditor may apply ex parte for an interim garnishee order upon producing an affidavit showing that his judgment is unsatisfied and that some person is indebted to the judgment debtor. The order provides that all debts "owing or accruing" from the third person (the garnishee) to the judgment debtor be attached to answer the judgment debt. Garnishee orders, like writs of execution, can be applied for only after a judgment is obtained. Under the Wages Act, 80 percent of the wages of "any mechanic, workman, laborer, servant, clerk or employee" is exempt from attachment (garnishment). However, the Judge making the order may reduce or increase the exemption under certain circumstances.

(d) Equitable Execution

Equitable execution is a form of relief granted by the court by appointment of a Receiver when legal execution, although available, could be ineffective. For example, it can be used to free exigible assets from impediments in the way of legal execution when they prevent the sheriff from seizing them. Legal execution must be impractical or unavailable as a result of such impediments; mere inconvenience of an available remedy is insufficient reason for appointing a Receiver. The relief granted by the court is the appointment of a Receiver of the particular property involved under the authority (in Ontario)of Section 114 of the Courts of Justice Act.

6. SOURCES OF LAW

(a) Statutory Law

(i) Company Law

Corporations are governed by one of the following legislations:

Federal:	Canada Business Corporations Act S.C. 1974-75-76, c. 33
Alberta:	Business Corporations Act, R.S.A. 1980, c. B-15
British Columbia:	Company Act, R.S. B.C. 1979, c. 59
Manitoba:	Corporations Act, S.M. 1976, c.40
New Brunswick:	Companies Act, R.S.N.B. 1973, c. C-13
Newfoundland:	The Corporations Act, S.N. 1986, c.12
Nova Scotia:	Companies Act R.S.N.S., 1967, c.42
Ontario:	Business Corporations Act, 1982, S.O. 1982,c.4
P.E.I.:	Companies Act, R.S.P.E.I. 1974, c. C-15
Quebec:	Companies Act, R.S.Q, 1977, c. C-38
Saskatchewan:	The Business Corporations Act, R.S.S. 1978, c. B-10

(ii) Winding Up

The law relating to winding up of companies is contained in:

Federal:	Winding-Up Act, R.S.C. 1970, c. W-10
New Brunswick:	Winding-Up Act, R.S.N.S., 1973, c. W-10
Nova Scotia:	Companies Winding-Up Act, R.S.N.S., 1967, c.47
P.E.I.:	Winding-Up Act, R.S.P.E.I., 1974, c. W-7
Quebec:	Winding-Up Act, R.S.Q. 1877, c. L-4
Saskatchewan:	The Companies Winding-up Act. R.S.S. 1978, c. C-24

(iii) Bankruptcy/Insolvency

The Canada Act allocates legislative power between the federal and provincial governments. Bankruptcy is a federal matter, so the Bankruptcy Act (R.S.C. 1970, c. B-3 as amended) and the general rules under the Bankruptcy Act (C.R.C. 1978, c 368 as amended) apply to the whole country. However, because"property and civil rights" are a provincial concern, numerous provincial laws also affect the conduct of a bankrupt's affairs.

In addition, in those particular circumstances mentioned in section 2.3 above, the Company Creditors Arrangement Act (R.S.C. 1970 C. C-25) may be applied to insolvency situations.

(b) Case Law

In addition to statute law, many fundamental principles of company and insolvency law are based on cases decided in the courts. Copies of decided cases are easily obtainable through major libraries or professional bodies. All civil courts are bound by the principle of legal precedent and are obliged to follow previous decisions of equivalent and higher courts. Decided cases are identified by the initials of the law report in which they are contained and by page number and year.

(c) Pending Developments

On January 28, 1986, the federal Minister of Consumer and Corporate Affairs, released the report of the Advisory Committee on Bankruptcy and Insolvency. It proposed important new amendments to the Bankruptcy Act that will significantly affect credit granting policies, realizing assets, and discharging liabilities in an insolvency or bankruptcy situation. However, the supporting legislation has not yet been introduced in the House of Commons.

7. SOURCES OF INFORMATION

(a) Administration of Company Law

The departments responsible for administering the respective corporations/companies Acts and the addresses where incorporating documents are kept are:

Federal: — Department of Consumer and Corporate Affairs

Director, Corporations Branch
Place du Portage
Hull, Quebec
K1A 0C9

Alberta: — Department of Consumer and Corporate Affairs

Registrar of Companies
Department of Consumer and Corporate Affairs
2nd Floor, Century Place
9803 — 102A Avenue
Edmonton, Alberta
T5J 3A3

British
Columbia: — Ministry of Consumer and Corporate Affairs

Registrar of Companies
Ministry of Consumer and Corporate Affairs
2nd Floor, 940 Blanchard Street
Victoria, B.C.
V8W 3E6

Manitoba: — Department of Consumer and Corporate Affairs
and Environment

Executive Director of Corporations and Business
Name Registration
10th Floor, 405 Broadway Avenue
Winnipeg, Manitoba
R3C 3L6

New Brunswick: — Department of Justice
Director, Corporations Branch
Consumer and Corporate Affairs
Department of Justice
Centennial Buildings
P.O. Box 6000
Fredericton, New Brunswick
E3B 5H1

Newfoundland — Department of Justice

Registrar of Deeds, Companies, and Securities
Department of Justice

Department of Justice
Confederation Building
St. John's, Newfoundland
A1C 5T7

Nova Scotia: — Department of the Attorney General

Registrar of Companies
Department of the Attorney General
1660 Hollis Street
Box 1529, Centennial Building
Halifax, Nova Scotia
B3J 2Y4

Ontario: — Ministry of Consumer and Commercial Relations

Companies Division
Ministry of Consumer and Commercial Relations
555 Yonge Street
Toronto, Ontario
M7A 2A6

P.E.I.:   — Department of Justice

Director of Corporations
Department of Justice
Provincial Administration Buildings
P.O. Box 2000
Charlottetown, Prince Edward Island
C1A 7N8

Quebec: — Ministry of Consumer Affairs, Cooperatives, and
                        Financial Institutions

Director of Companies/Direction des Compagnies
Ministry of Consumer Affairs, Cooperatives, and
Financial Institutions/
Ministere des Consommateurs Cooperatives et
Institutions financieres
806, Place d'Youville, 5e etage
Quebec City, Quebec
G1R 4T5

Saskatchewan   — Department of Consumer and Commercial Affairs

Director of Corporations
Department of Consumer and Commercial Affairs
1919 Rose Street
Regina, Saskatchewan
S4P 3V7

(b) Access to Corporate Records

Corporate Records Requirements by Jurisdiction

Jurisdiction	What	Who	Conditions
1. Federal Manitoba Saskatchewan Newfoundland	Articles, bylaws, unanimous shareholder agreement, minutes and resolutions of shareholders, notices, securities, register list of shareholders	Shareholder, creditor, director plus their agents and legal representatives	-During normal business hours -Appropriate request required for shareholders list -No fee
2. Federal Manitoba (distributing corporation only) Saskatchewan	Articles, bylaws, unanimous shareholder agreement, minutes and resolutions of shareholders, notices, securities, register, list of shareholders	Any person	-During normal business hours -Reasonable fee
3. Ontario	Articles, bylaws, unanimous shareholder agreement, minutes and resolutions of shareholders, register of directors, list of shareholders, register of directors, list of shareholders	Shareholder, creditor, director plus their agents and legal representatives	-During normal business hours -Appropriate request required for shareholders list -No fee
4. Ontario	Articles, bylaws, unanimous shareholder agreement, minutes and resolutions of shareholders, register of directors, list of shareholders, register of directors, list of shareholders	Any person	-During normal business hours -Appropriate request required for shareholders list -Reasonable fee
5. Ontario	Articles, bylaws, unanimous shareholder agreement, minutes and resolutions of shareholders, register of directors, list of shareholders, register of directors, securities register, accounting records, minutes and resolutions of directors and committees	Directors	-During normal business hours
6. Alberta New Brunswick	Articles, bylaws, unanimous shareholder agreement, (and amendments) minutes and resolutions of shareholders, notices, securities register, financial statements, register of disclosures, list of shareholders	Shareholder, directors plus their agents and legal representatives	-During normal business hours -Appropriate request required for shareholders list -No fee

7. Alberta	Register of mortgages	Any person, creditor, member, Alberta company	-During normal business hours unless articles limit to two consecutive hours per day -Reasonable fee
8. Alberta New Brunswick	Unanimous shareholder agreement, articles, bylaws, notices, securities register, list of shareholders	Creditors and their agents and legal representatives	-During normal business hours -Appropriate request required for shareholders list -Reasonable fee
9. Alberta	Notices, securities register, list of shareholders	Any Person	-During normal business hours -Appropriate request required for shareholders list -Reasonable fee
10. British Columbia	Corporate records and accounting records	Past and present directors	-During normal business hours
11. British Columbia	Most corporate records as seen in section 187(2) of the Act and accounting records	Members	-During normal business hours but may be restricted by ordinary resolution to two consecutive hours per day -Accounting records subject to conditions imposed by directors
12. British Columbia (reporting company only)	Some corporate records as seen in section 187(3) of Act	Any person	-During normal business hours but may be restricted by ordinary resolution to two consecutive hours per day -Reasonable fee
13. British Columbia (nonreporting company)	Limited corporate records as seen in section 187(4) of Act	Any person	-During normal business hours but may be restricted by ordinary resolution to two consecutive hours per day -Reasonable fee
14. Prince Edward Island	Corporate records maintained at head office	Shareholders, creditors and their legal representatives	-During normal business hours

funds under the Employment Protection (Consolidation) Act 1978.

(v) Claims for money advanced to pay wages or salaries to the same extent to which the employees who have been paid would have been preferential under (iv) above if the money had not been so advanced.

(vi) Various miscellaneous taxes.

If there are insufficient funds to pay all the preferential creditors in full, they are paid pari passu.

(e) <u>Creditors secured by a floating charge</u> The nature of a floating charge is described in §4.7 and the receivership procedure is described in §2.4. The debenture-holder may be paid only out of the proceeds of the assets secured by the debenture after taking into account the cost of realizing the assets, the costs of winding up, and the claims of the preferential creditors.

Any surplus remaining after discharging the debenture-holder is available to the unsecured creditors.

(f) <u>Unsecured creditors</u> When all preferential creditors have been paid in full and the amounts due to any debenture-holders secured by a floating charge have also been paid, the remaining funds are distributed pari passu among the remaining unsecured creditors.

(g) <u>Claims for postliquidation interest</u> Interest that has accrued prior to the liquidation date on debts may be included in the claims of the creditors noted above. However, interest accruing after the date of liquidation ranks behind the unsecured creditors' claims.

(h) <u>Amount of claim</u> The amount of claim is subject to the following:

(i) The claim is for the contractual amount due, subject to any mitigating factors to reflect the actual loss suffered by the creditor.

(ii) If the claim is interest-bearing and secured, interest up to the date that the security is realized is normally paid in full, to the extent to which the security is adequate to cover the claim including interest. If the claim is interest-bearing but not secured, creditors may add the interest which accrued prior to the liquidation date to their claims, and make a further claim in respect of interest which has accrued since the date of liquidation. If before liquidation a creditor whose debt carries no contractual interest gives notice to the company that interest will be charged, it can be claimed at the lesser of the rate demanded and the rate payable under Section 17 of the Judgment Act 1938 (currently 15%). Postliquidation interest under subparagraph g is calculated on the greater of the Judgment Act rate and the contractual rate (if any), unless the contractual rate is found to be extortionate.

(iii) Claims in currencies other than sterling are converted into sterling at the rate of exchange quoted at the liquidation date.

(iv) Creditors may not include the legal costs incurred in pursuing their claims,

Hardy, Anne E., "Crown Priority in Insolvency," Carswell, 1986.

Houlden, Lloyd, W. and C.H. Morawetz, "Bankruptcy Law of Canada." Toronto, Carswell 1960-. 2 vols. Loose leaf current service.

McGill University, Faculty of Law, "Bankruptcy — Present Problems and Future Perspectives," De Boo, 1986.

Springman, M.A. and Gertner, E. "Debtor-Creditor Law, Practice & Doctrine." Buttersworth, 1985.

Law Reports:

Canadian Bankruptcy Reports Annotated. Toronto, Carswell 1920-.(1st Ser.): vols. 1-38, 1920-1960; new ser.: vol. 1 1960-

Periodicals:

Insolvency Bulletin, Vol. 1, 1980-. Ottawa, Office of the Superintendent of Bankruptcy, Dept. of Consumer and Corporate Affairs, 1980-.

Construction Liens:

Kirsh, H.J. "A Guide of Construction Liens in Ontario." Scarborough, Ont., Butterworths, 1984.

Law Society of Upper Canada. Continuing Legal Education."Construction Lien Act, 1983." Toronto, The Society, 1983.

Personal Property Security:

McLaren, Richard H. "Secured Transactions in Personal Property in Canada." Toronto, Carswell, 1979-. 2 vols. Loose Leaf.

Law Reports

"Personal Property Security Act Cases." Vol. 1 1977/81-. Toronto, Carswell, 1982- (Forms part of McLaren's "Secured Transactions in Personal Property in Canada." Also issued separately).

Receivers:

Bennett, Frank "Receiverships," Carswell, 1985.

Bristow, D.I. and MacKlen, D.N. "Mechanics Liens in Canada." Toronto, Carswell.

UNITED KINGDOM

United Kingdom
Table of Contents

UNITED KINGDOM

NOTE ON LEGAL SYSTEMS AND PROCEDURES IN THE UNITED KINGDOM

The United Kingdom comprises Great Britain (England and Wales, and Scotland), and Northern Ireland. The information in this book is based primarily on the law of England and Wales; references to 'England' include Wales.

The law of Scotland is fundamentally different from that of England and Wales; but statute has tended to approximate one to the other. Corporate insolvency procedures differ little; individual insolvency procedures more substantially. Where Scots law shows significant differences from English, this has been noted in the text. The law of Northern Ireland is less dissimilar from that of England, but, again, any material differences are noted.

INSOLVENCY PRACTITIONERS

The Insolvency Act 1986 provides that only an authorized insolvency practitioner may have the conduct of any insolvency proceedings, including the winding up of a solvent company. He will normally be an accountant. The Department of Trade and Industry recognizes certain professional bodies for the purpose of their granting authorizations to those who are subject to their disciplinary procedures. Most authorizations are granted by these bodies. They are: the main accountancy bodies, the Insolvency Practitioners Association and the Law Societies. Authorization may also be obtained from the Secretary of State for Trade and Industry. An insolvency practitioner is required to have an insurance bond, generally and in respect of each appointment.

An authorized insolvency practitioner may not act in respect of any insolvent company where he, or his firm, have had a previous professional or reporting arrangement unconnected with the insolvency proceedings within the previous two years.

1. TYPES OF BUSINESS ENTITY

There are few restrictions on which legal form a business may adopt. The vast majority of significant business enterprises in the United Kingdom are limited companies with share capital. These are now governed primarily in Great Britain by the

Companies Act 1985, and their insolvency by the Insolvency Act 1986. These Acts are as applicable to large public companies with many shareholders as to small private companies with only two or three shareholders. Although there are differences between public and private companies, they are the same type of legal entity.

Businesses are entitled to trade under names that are not those of their proprietors, but must in general disclose their proprietors' true names and addresses in all business documents and at all places of business.

1.1 Limited Companies

A limited company is a legal entity distinct from its shareholders; it can own property, and sue and be sued in its own name. In the event of the company's insolvency, a shareholder's liability is limited to any unpaid portion of the nominal value of his shareholding. In practice it is rare for there to be any such 'uncalled' share capital, except in certain new businesses.

The company is bound by its Memorandum and Articles of Association, which define respectively its objects and constitution and its internal regulations. Most companies adopt a standard form or a variation of it based upon the officially published 'Table A.' European Community legislation has removed the effects of most limitations imposed on the powers of companies by their articles, so far as their dealings with the outside world are concerned.

Limited companies may be either public or private. A public company incorporates the words 'public limited company' or the abbreviation 'p.l.c.' in its name. A private company has the word 'limited' (often abbreviated to 'ltd.') as part of its name. Occasionally, a company may get a special dispensation from the Registrar of Companies not to have the words 'limited' or 'p.l.c.' as part of its formal name.

Some, but by no means all, public companies may have their shares traded freely (or 'listed') on a Stock Exchange or under various similar arrangements. Under these arrangements, often called 'listing agreements', they have to make additional information available to the public; and the agreements commonly impose restrictions on the powers of directors that can only be lifted by the shareholders.

From the point of view of insolvency procedures, there are no practical differences between public and private companies.

The other main distinguishing features between public and private companies include the following:

(a) The stocks and shares of a public company may be freely issued to the public (subject only to statutes protecting the public at large) and there can be no restrictions on their transfer. Private companies may not issue stock to the public at large and may incorporate restrictions on transfers to anyone other than existing shareholders (these are normally referred to as preemption rights and are incorporated in the Articles of Association).

(b) A public company's minimum issued share capital is £50,000, of which at least 25% must be paid up. Some restrictions apply to the issue of shares by a public company for a consideration other than cash. The minimum capital requirement for a private company is £2.

(c) A public company must call an extraordinary general meeting of shareholders if its accumulated losses exceed 50% of its issued share capital, although the company does not necessarily have to be wound up then. There is no such obligation on a private company.

(d) A public company must take account of both realized and unrealized losses before distributing its net current realized profits; a private company is not restricted in this way.

A company is managed by its board of directors appointed by the shareholders (a minimum of two for a public company, although a private company can have only one director if its Articles so provide). Employees have no power to appoint directors to the Board.

Independently audited financial statements must be filed by all limited companies with the Registrar of Companies, where they are available for inspection by the public. However, small and medium-sized companies, as defined by the Companies Act 1985, need only file abridged accounts, with limited supporting information, rather than full accounts. Accounts must be filed within seven months of the accounting year end for public companies, and ten months for private companies. A company may decide on any convenient date for its year end ('Accounting reference date').

1.2 Partnerships

A partnership (sometimes referred to as a firm) is not considered at law as a legal entity distinct from its individual partners (except in Scotland). Each partner is jointly (and, in Scotland, severally) liable for all contractual debts and obligations incurred by the partnership; and jointly and severally liable in respect of other liabilities. It is possible to form a limited partnership, where some of the partners (not involved in management) have limited liability, but this is rarely done because it is generally more convenient to incorporate a limited company.

A partnership must comprise at least two partners but not more than twenty, except in the case of banks and certain professions. The constitution of a partnership is normally set out in a deed of agreement between the partners, but there is no legal requirement for this. A partnership does not have a share capital, and the legal interest in a partnership is not generally transferable. Partnerships are not required to publish their financial statements, nor (except for limited partnerships) to be registered in any central registry.

Partnerships are usually either:

(a) practitioners of professions whose professional rules do not allow the liability of the members to be limited; or

(b) small businesses that have not sought the protection of limited liability.

1.3 Sole Traders

An individual operating a business on his own account is referred to as a 'sole trader.' There are no requirements for registration in a central registry, or for public filing of financial statements.

1.4 Other Business Entities

There are other more specialist business entities, including:

(a) 'friendly' and 'provident' societies;

(b) public corporations governed by individual Acts of Parliament or Royal Charters;

(c) companies limited by guarantee; and

(d) charitable organizations.

These are rarely the subject of insolvency proceedings and specialist advice should be sought in the event of the insolvency of any of them.

2. REORGANIZATION PROCEDURES

The procedures to be followed in the reorganization of limited companies differ from those applicable to individuals and partnerships, although in some instances the same terminology is used. It is essential therefore for a creditor to establish the legal status of his debtor. The reorganization procedures in this chapter are those applicable to limited companies. The two principal procedures used to rehabilitate insolvent companies are receivership and administration.

A. Limited Companies

The normal reorganization procedures applicable to limited companies are:

(a) administration;

(b) voluntary arrangement under Part I of the Insolvency Act 1986;

(c) compromise or arrangement under the Companies Act 1985;

(d) administrative receivership; and

(e) informal arrangement.

Administrations and voluntary arrangements are dealt with together below in paragraph 2.1, as in practice voluntary arrangements outside administrations will be very rare.

Administrative receivership is, strictly speaking, a method of enforcing security granted by a floating charge over the debtor's assets, rather than a reorganization procedure. However, it is included in this section because receivership commonly operates to salvage an insolvent business, albeit under new ownership.

2.1 Administration — The administration procedure was introduced by the Insolvency Act 1986. It is a legal procedure that permits insolvent companies to be reorganized and refinanced. It may also be used to effect a better realization of assets than liquidation. This would include the repackaging of the business and sale.

The administrator is appointed by, and reports to, the Court. His powers and duties are set out in the Insolvency Act 1986 but may be amended or extended by the Court. The administrator manages the affairs of the company on behalf of all of its creditors. The purposes of the administration are set out in the petition for administration and are confirmed in the Court Order.

Administration may be only an interim arrangement to give a company protection from its creditors while it reorganizes itself. Alternatively, and more commonly, administration will be combined with a voluntary arrangement under the Insolvency Act whereby the creditors agree to compromise their claims.

The procedure is at all times under the control of the Court as it affects the rights of the creditors. In particular it restricts the rights of secured creditors, finance and leasing companies, and those who have supplied items to the company on terms retaining ownership pending payment.

2.1.1 Appointment of an Administrator — The company, its directors or any creditor may petition the Court for an Administration Order, directing that the company should be managed by an insolvency practitioner ('the administrator'). Commonly it will be the company that petitions, as a creditor will be unlikely to have adequate knowledge of the company's financial affairs. On service of the petition and prior to its hearing the company cannot enter into voluntary or compulsory liquidation nor can a creditor take any enforcement action without leave of the Court, with the single exception of a creditor secured by a floating charge (see §4.7). A creditor secured by a floating charge has to be served with notice of the petition and can appoint an administrative receiver. This right only remains open for a limited period (commonly five working days).

When the petition is presented, it may be accompanied by an accountant's report on the company's affairs. This will normally be prepared by the proposed administrator, and will set out the company's financial position and the purposes of the proposed administration. It will state that, in the reporting accountant's opinion, the purposes may be achieved.

The Court, upon hearing the petition, will make an Administration Order if it is satisfied that:

(1) the company is, or is likely to become, unable to pay its debts; and

(2) the Order is likely to achieve one or more of the following purposes:

    (a) the survival of the company as a going concern, together with the whole or any part of its business;

    (b) the approval of a voluntary arrangement under the Insolvency Act;

    (c) the sanctioning of a compromise under the Companies Act;

    (d) a better realization of the company's assets than a liquidation would be likely to achieve.

If an administrative receiver has been appointed by the floating chargeholder, no administrator can be appointed unless it appears that the charge was void.

The Court also cannot make an order if the company is already in liquidation, but a liquidator can seek a voluntary arrangement and rescue the business in that way.

When the Administration Order has been made, any preliminary moves already made toward liquidation proceed no further. In addition, receivers must vacate office (although their accrued remuneration will be protected). While the Order remains in force, the company cannot go into liquidation and no receiver can be appointed. No enforcement of security, or legal proceedings, can be taken against the company without the consent of the administrator or the Court.

2.1.2 Administrator's Powers — The administrator's powers are governed by the Insolvency Act 1986 and the Administration Order, and he has all the powers necessary to manage the affairs of the company. He takes control of the property - including charged property - and manages it according to the Act and the Court's directions until his plans are approved by a meeting of creditors. He can deal with assets subject to floating charges as though they were uncharged, and the costs incurred during his administration are paid in priority to debts secured by a floating charge.

The administrator may, with the sanction of the Court, also dispose of assets subject to fixed charges, or to hire purchase or similar agreements; or supplied under retention of title. The Court's consent will be given if the disposals are likely to promote the purpose of the Administration Order. When a disposal is made the secured creditor is entitled to the net proceeds of sale or the open market value (if greater).

An administrator has the power to remove and appoint directors, and to call meetings of the company or its creditors. Neither the company nor its officers may exercise powers that might interfere with the administrator's powers without his consent.

2.1.3 Administrator's Obligations — The administrator must notify the company's shareholders and creditors of his appointment and make statutory returns to the Registrar of Companies and advertise his appointment.

A meeting of creditors must be held within three months of the administrator's appointment. The shareholders and creditors have to be sent a statement of his proposals for achieving the purposes specified in the Administration Order (and a copy will also be sent to the Registrar of Companies). The creditors may approve these proposals or make any modification to which the administrator consents. The meeting may also appoint a committee of creditors, which has the right to call for ex· planations and information from the administrator. The administrator must notify the Court and all interested parties of the results of the meeting.

In the event that the creditors do not approve the administrator's proposals, the Court may discharge the Administration Order or make any other Order it thinks fit, including overriding the creditors' views. If the administrator wishes to revise or update his proposals, he must call a further meeting of creditors and obtain their approval to the variations. He must apply to the Court to have the original order varied or discharged if either he achieves the purposes specified in the Order or it becomes clear to him that they cannot be achieved.

If any person believes that the administrator's management of the company or disposal of assets is unfairly prejudicial to his interest, he may apply to the Court for relief. Any relief that will prejudice the administrator's proposals has to be requested within the four weeks after those proposals have been approved by the creditors.

While the Administration Order is in force, the administrator is deemed to be the agent of the company. His obligations to affected parties, both those at the date of his appointment and those arising during the administration, are governed by his proposals. His contractual debts and liabilities, as well as his remuneration and expenses, are charged on the assets of the company (excluding fixed charge assets).

If the administrator considers that an immediate liquidation would produce no distribution to unsecured creditors of the company, he may issue a Certificate of Insolvency. Creditors will then be able to obtain Bad Debt Relief on the Value Added Tax portion of their claims.

2.1.4 Voluntary Arrangement — One of the possible purposes of an administration is the approval of a 'voluntary arrangement' with the company's creditors. This is a statutory compromise supervised by an authorized insolvency practitioner. Because of inherent risks of control during the formulation of a scheme, few voluntary arrangements will be attempted without the company's first entering into administration. The scheme is also available to a liquidator but will be used less in such circumstances: liquidation would never be preferred as a route to a voluntary arrangement.

Meetings of all the company's creditors and shareholders are convened on at least 14 days' notice. The creditors and shareholders must be sent prior to this meeting a package comprising:

(i) the proposal for the voluntary arrangement;

(ii) a statement of affairs showing the company's assets and liabilities, and their respective priorities.

There must also be an indication of the advantages to creditors of supporting a voluntary arrangement. The proposal should include details of the company's business activities and supporting information. New finance may be introduced into the company in cash or in forgiveness of debt.

This package will be sent out by an authorized insolvency practitioner, who for these purposes will be called the 'nominee.' It is his responsibility to satisfy himself and the creditors that the voluntary arrangement is commercially viable.

The proposal will normally provide a formula for the compromise of creditors' claims. A voluntary arrangement operates either as a composition in satisfaction of the company's debts or as a scheme of arrangement of its affairs. A composition is an agreement between the company and its creditors that they will accept an orderly repayment of part of what they are owed in satisfaction of the whole. This may be guaranteed by a third party. The supervisor of the voluntary arrangement oversees the implementation of the composition, but does not become trustee.

In a scheme of arrangement the supervisor becomes trustee of the company's property. A scheme is a suitable vehicle for a compromise considerably more sophisticated than a composition. For instance, it might include conversion of liabilities to equity or loan stock, and injection of outside capital. It may include a future profit share for creditors. Either a composition or a scheme of arrangement can be used to enable an insolvent company with potential to make a fresh start; but either can also be used to achieve an orderly winding down of a company's affairs, with higher distributions to unsecured creditors than they would receive on a winding up.

The creditors will vote on the proposals, and may amend them. A majority of three-quarters, by value of claims, of the creditors who vote (in person or by proxy) at the meetings, must vote in favor of the proposals. Each secured or preferential creditor has a veto over the loss of its rights. Shareholders must approve by simple majority.

The results of the meetings and the approval of the creditors and shareholders is reported to the Court. There is then a 28-day period during which any creditor or interested party may petition the Court to object to the proposed scheme. They need to show that they have been unfairly prejudiced by the proposals. This may be difficult to prove.

The Court will then approve the voluntary arrangement proposals, following which they will be binding upon all creditors and shareholders who were notified of them. It is not clear whether any persons who were accidentally not notified will be bound by the proposals since there has, as yet, been no case law on the subject.

On the approval by the creditors of the proposals, the nominee will become the supervisor of the scheme and will be responsible for its operation. As he will commonly be the same person as the administrator of the company, the handover will be smooth. If the approval of the Voluntary Arrangement completes the achievement of the Administrator's purposes, he will apply to the Court for the discharge of the Administration Order.

Implementation of the proposals may result in the rehabilitation of the company itself, leaving behind its former creditors and the approved financial package. Alternatively, it will leave the company as a shell, which may be liquidated or dissolved.

2.1.5 Termination of the Administration — When the administrator has completed his tasks, he applies to the Court for the discharge of the Administration Order, and this will be effective from the date specified by the Court. The administrator must notify the Registrar of Companies when discharged.

The Court, on discharging the Administration Order, will make further Orders to provide for what should follow. If the company has survived, it may be handed back to the directors, who may be new directors appointed by the administrator. If the purpose of the Administration Order was to obtain the approval of a voluntary arrangement, the administrator will hand over to the supervisor of the arrangement (this will probably be a technical handover as the supervisor will commonly be the same person). However, if the Administration Order was to achieve a greater realization than could be obtained through a liquidation, it is then probable that a winding-up Order will be made in order to distribute the assets to the creditors. The administrator can become the liquidator, and the liquidation effectively backdates to the date of the original order. If that purpose, however, was combined with that of the approval of a voluntary arrangement to wind the company down in an orderly fashion, the administrator would remain in post as supervisor until the realization and distribution was over, when the company could be dissolved.

2.2 Compromise or Arrangement — Prior to the introduction of the administration procedure, a compromise or arrangement under Section 425 of the Companies Act 1985 was the only enforceable method of reorganization where receivership was not available and liquidation was inappropriate. The sanctioning of such a scheme is one of the possible purposes of an administration. The permission of the court is required, and a majority in number representing 75% in value of each class of creditors and shareholders must approve the scheme. The court determines the classes, and each class has to have a separate meeting to approve the scheme.

The procedures are cumbersome and expensive in professional costs. They are also high risk, in that there is uncertainty as to outcome because success is dependent upon substantial goodwill and faith by a very high proportion of the company's creditors.

While the scheme is being put into effect, the company is not protected from individual action by any creditor, unless sheltered by an administration order. Very few corporate schemes are attempted and fewer are a success. It is expected that voluntary arrangements will almost entirely replace such schemes in cases of insolvency, except in cases in which a complex structure of different classes of creditor (for instance, loan stock creditors) renders the approval of a voluntary arrangement by a single creditors' meeting inappropriate because it is too easily challenged in the courts.

A structural reorganization of a company or group of companies (often for tax planning purposes) may also be effected under Sections 110 and 111 of the Insolvency Act 1986. This procedure only affects the shareholders, although in theory it can be used in an insolvent liquidation. It does not normally require the sanction of the court.

Voluntary arrangements under Part 1 of the Insolvency Act 1986 can be effected outside of formal insolvency but would not commonly be so except in special circumstances, because of the lack of protection during the organizational period. Voluntary arrangements are commonly linked with administration. Details of a voluntary arrangement are therefore set out in § 2.1.4.

2.3 Administrative Receivership — An administrative receivership is not strictly a reorganization procedure. It is a statutorily controlled procedure whereby the unpaid holder of a floating charge debenture appoints an administrative receiver ('receiver') to take control of and manage the charged assets. The charged assets commonly comprise the whole of the company's business and assets, subject to the prior fixed charge rights of other secured creditors (and the rights of suppliers under hire purchase, lease, or retention of title).

The effect of the appointment is that the business and assets are removed from the control of the company. Creditors may not enforce judgments against those assets although they can still petition for the winding up of the company. A resultant liquidator is, however, in no better position and has to 'wait in the wings' until the receiver has finished with his assignment. The only practical effect of liquidation during the conduct of a receivership is that it terminates the receiver's power to act as agent of the company. Thereafter he operates either as principal or as agent of the debenture holder. The debenture holder may thus become liable for the actions of the receiver.

Receivership can normally be instituted by a debenture-holder on demand and without prior notice to the company, if the debenture so provides (it commonly does). Because the receiver has power to trade and dispose of the company's assets as a going concern, it is one of the most important methods by which medium and large-sized companies are, in effect, reorganized and the means by which the business or trade (as opposed to the legal entity) of many insolvent companies is allowed to continue.

Although floating charge debentures may be granted to any creditor to secure indebtedness, in practice they are most commonly used by banks as a means of securing the ordinary bank overdraft and short term lending by which many British companies are financed. The terms of most debentures and lending agreements provide for repayment on demand in certain circumstances (in particular if the security for the lending is in jeopardy). Failure to repay on demand can result in the immediate appointment of a receiver.

Although it may seem drastic for a bank to have these powers it is generally found that the banks only take such action when the company is in a terminal condition. The appointment of a receiver is generally considered to be in the interest of all creditors and not just of the appointing bank because the receiver is commonly able to achieve better overall realizations by selling the business as a going concern than would occur if it were shut down and the assets disposed of piecemeal.

2.3.1 Appointment of a Receiver — An administrative receiver is appointed under a deed of appointment by a floating chargeholder, usually following formal demand for repayment of the lending. The debtor company has no choice as to the identity of the insolvency practitioner who is appointed.

Receivers can also be appointed under fixed charges or mortgages on property, or by an order of the court. These are not reorganizational appointments and are therefore dealt with in § 3.

The receiver's powers and duties are governed by the Insolvency Act 1986 and by the provisions of the relevant mortgage deed or debenture. In practice, most debentures are taken by banks to secure lending to customer companies, and the wording of the debenture follows a standard and comprehensive form. The debenture is usually expressed to secure 'all monies due' and not merely a fixed sum. This should not be confused with the issue of a debenture loan stock, which is a marketable security, securing a specific sum of money. In this case, a trustee (commonly an insurance company), is usually appointed for the debenture holders, and the provisions of the trust deed govern the conditions under which the debentures may be enforced.

If a company commences to be wound up, or a successful administration petition is presented against it, within twelve months of the creation of a floating charge granted to secure existing indebtedness, the charge will be invalid, except to the extent of any fresh, or 'new,' monies advanced during the period. An exception to this is if it can be proved that the company was solvent immediately after the granting of such a charge. This is often difficult.

This provision serves to defeat the attempts of creditors to obtain additional security from companies in financial difficulties to the detriment of other unsecured creditors. It does not, however, enable any repayment of the secured debt to be recovered.

When a charge is granted to a person 'connected' with the company (a director or shareholder, or someone associated with them), then the period during which the charge may be rendered invalid becomes two years.

2.3.2 Receiver's Powers — The receiver's powers are determined by statute and by the mortgage deed or debenture. These normally confer on the receiver the right to manage the company's assets and to realize them as he sees fit. Consequently, the receiver will take over all the directors' powers of management. If possible he will continue the company's trade, at least for a short time after his appointment, while he assesses the viability of the business.

Sometimes, when the receiver decides to continue trading for a period, he may, for protective reasons, transfer the business and certain tangible assets to a newly-incorporated subsidiary company. This process is known as 'hiving down,' and does not affect the interests of the debtor company's creditors. Under these arrangements, no consideration for the transfer is paid immediately. It is calculated when, and if, the business and assets are ultimately sold to a third party.

If the receiver sells the business as a going concern, the purchaser normally buys the assets free of any encumbrance or obligation to pay the insolvent company's creditors. Exceptions will be where assets are legally owned by third parties (such as goods supplied on hire purchase or lease or subject to retention of title). Here the receiver will either arrange for the third party's claim to be settled, or the obligation will be transferred and the sale price adjusted.

The assets sold by a receiver will normally only comprise the tangible assets, goodwill, and property rights relevant to the ongoing business.

The receiver will retain, and collect, the company's receivables and will separately dispose of any other assets not required by a purchaser. The company's employees will commonly be discharged by the receiver and the purchaser may reemploy, without any accrued employment rights, those members of the staff and workforce he requires.

A receiver may apply to the Court to sell property charged by a prior charge to someone other than his appointor. If the fixed charge creditor is not going to be paid in full, the receiver needs to show that this course of action is essential to promote a favorable realization of all the company's assets. The person to whom the property is charged will be entitled to the greater of the net proceeds of the disposal and the open market value, as determined by the Court.

2.3.3 Receiver's Obligations — The receiver must notify the company and all creditors of his appointment. In addition, he is required to advertise his appointment and make certain statutory returns. However, he is not obliged to ensure that the company complies with such statutory requirements as filing annual financial statements with the Registrar of Companies, and commonly these requirements are allowed to lapse.

The officers of the company must provide the receiver with a statement of the company's affairs, showing its assets and liabilities. The statutory time limit for this is twenty-one days but normally substantial extensions are granted.

Within three months of his appointment, the receiver must report to the Registrar of Companies and the creditors on the events leading up to his appointment, the disposal of the company's assets, the liabilities of the company, and the estimated amounts payable to the different classes of creditor. The report includes a summary of the statement of affairs and of any comments the receiver has on it. A meeting of creditors, at which this report will be presented, may establish a committee to monitor the progress of the receivership. However, this committee does not have any powers to control the receiver's conduct.

The receiver is not liable for the debts of the company incurred before his appointment, nor is he bound to adopt any of the contractual obligations of the company. When obligations become due after the date of his appointment, providing that he does not adopt the contract under which the liability arises, any such claim ranks merely as an unsecured claim against the company.

The receiver may even exclude personal liability for supplies or services provided to the company that were confirmed or ordered by him or on his authority. Payment for those supplies and services, however, takes priority over any other use of receivership funds; and no reputable insolvency practitioner would leave such suppliers unpaid. Creditors should, therefore, ensure that any goods supplied to a company after a receiver's appointment are supplied against orders made in the name of the receiver.

A receiver is not required to deal with the claims of unsecured creditors, If, however, he forms the opinion that they will not receive a dividend on their claims, he may issue a Certificate of Insolvency and notify the creditors accordingly. They will then be able to obtain full repayment from HM Customs & Excise in respect of any Value Added Tax element in their claims.

Following the disposal of the assets, the receiver will apportion the net proceeds (after taking into account the costs of receivership, including his own remuneration) between:

(a) fixed charge assets; and

(b) floating charge assets,

as defined by statute and the mortgage debenture.

The receiver pays the net sale proceeds of the assets covered by the fixed charge direct to the debenture-holder. However, before he distributes the net funds covered by the floating charge, he must first pay the preferential creditors (see §3.2.6a). In practice, liabilities to these creditors are likely to be substantial, and the agreement of their claims, particularly those of the Inland Revenue and Customs & Excise (tax authorities), tends to delay substantially the completion of many receiverships.

The receiver's remuneration is approved by the debenture-holder, but it is paid, in priority, out of the assets of the company in receivership.

2.3.4 Termination of the Receivership — When the receiver has paid the preferential creditors out of the floating charge assets and accounted to the debenture-holder for the balance of those assets (if any) and any amounts due under a fixed charge, he must account to the company. Normally, by that time a liquidator would have been appointed and the receiver will account to him.

The receivership is terminated when the debenture-holder grants the receiver his release. The receiver must notify the Registrar of Companies when he ceases to act.

2.4 Informal Arrangement — Outside the statutory insolvency procedures, major creditors may individually and collectively agree to defer taking action against the debtor company on the grounds that their interest will be better served by permitting it to continue trading. The agreement to forbear from enforcing obligations is called a moratorium.

This may particularly be the case if the debtor company is apparently only in temporary financial difficulties. For example, the company may have been overtrading and have assets locked up in contracts which, if realization was required urgently, would result in substantial loss. A controlled unwinding or refinancing program could, on the other hand, result in beneficial recoveries to the creditors.

The administration procedures of the Insolvency Act 1986 will have almost certainly replaced the need for informal schemes. Indeed one of the principal purposes of the appointment of an administrator is to permit 'the survival of the company ... as a going concern.'

Even in cases in which almost universal creditor goodwill renders the total protection of an administration unnecessary, it is now unlikely that creditors will forego the more limited protection afforded by a voluntary arrangement and proceed entirely outside the Insolvency Act.

3. TERMINAL PROCEDURES

As with reorganization procedures, no distinction is made between trading and nontrading companies. The terminal procedures relating to limited companies do differ from those relating to partnerships, sole traders, and private individuals.

A. Definition of Insolvency

A company is insolvent when it is unable to pay its debts as and when they fall due. This can be apparent when, for instance, judgment debts remain unsatisfied or checks are returned unpaid by the company's bankers.

A company is also insolvent when its liabilities, including its contingent and prospective liabilities, exceed the value of its assets. This is known as the 'asset test.'

B. Types of Liquidation Procedure—Striking Off

The term 'liquidation' is more commonly used than the statutory term 'winding up' to denote the process whereby a limited company's assets are realized and the company dissolved. The terms have the same meaning.

There are three principal types of liquidation procedure, as follows:

(a) Members' voluntary (or solvent) liquidation, in which all debts are paid in full and shareholders receive a return on the capital they have subscribed. The directors make a formal declaration of solvency.

(b) Creditors' voluntary liquidation, in which the shareholders and the creditors of an insolvent company appoint a liquidator, without direct interference or control from either the court or Government departments.

(c) Winding up by the Court (commonly known in England and Wales as compulsory liquidation), following an application (or petition) to the Court by an affected party. This type of liquidation is supervised by the Court and the Department of Trade and Industry.

Of the two types of insolvent liquidation, a creditors' voluntary liquidation is usually more advantageous to creditors than a compulsory liquidation, from the point of view of both cost and time. Generally, unless creditors wish the Official Receiver to investigate the affairs of the insolvent company, or have reason to believe that the liquidator chosen may not be impartial, it is usually in their interest to support a creditors' voluntary liquidation and not to insist upon a compulsory liquidation.

A company may also be dissolved informally without the need for liquidation procedures if it is dormant and has no assets or liabilities. An application is made by the directors to the Register of Companies inviting him to strike the company from the Registrar of Companies. The Registrar will make enquiries of the various statutory authorities and Inland Revenue and will publish notice of the proposed dissolution in the appropriate gazette. The company is dissolved three months thereafter but can be restored to the Register by application to Court at any time in the following twenty years. Normally, a year to eighteen months elapses between the time of application to the Registrar and the publishing of the notice.

On occasion, the Registrar will decide himself that a company is defunct (commonly if he has received no annual returns for several years). He may write to the last known directors and the registered office stating that he proposes to strike the company off unless he hears to the contrary.

In either respect, the directors' statutory duties and responsibilities continue up until the dissolution. This includes the obligation to prepare and file annual accounts.

If a company is struck off the register, any interested party may apply within the following 20 years to have it restored.

3.1 Members' Voluntary Liquidation — A members' voluntary liquidation assumes that the company is solvent and all its debts will be paid in full. The reason for winding up is usually one of the following:

(a) the corporate structure is to be reorganized;

(b) the business in question has been sold or closed down and the shareholders want to recover their capital; or

(c) the purpose for which the company was formed has ceased to exist or is no longer capable of achievement.

3.1.1 Commencement of the Proceedings — The procedures are as follows:

(a) The directors meet and resolve to recommend that the company be wound up and that a liquidator (or liquidators) be appointed; they convene a meeting of shareholders to give effect to these decisions.

(b) A majority of the directors must make a statutory 'declaration of solvency,' witnessed by a solicitor, confirming that they believe the company will be able to pay all its debts within twelve months of the commencement of the winding up. The declaration of solvency is supported by a schedule of the company's assets and liabilities, prepared as at the latest practical date.

(c) The declaration of solvency must be made not more than five weeks before the shareholders' meeting, and must be lodged with the Registrar of Companies not later than fifteen days after the passing of the shareholders' resolution to liquidate.

(d) The shareholders meet and pass a special resolution that the company be wound up and a named liquidator appointed. To pass the resolution, at least 75% of the votes cast at the meeting (in person or by proxy) must be in favor. Following this resolution, the liquidator is the sole officer of the company and the powers of the directors cease. The company's legal existence, however, continues until it is dissolved.

(e) The liquidator must file notice of his appointment with the Registrar of Companies and advertise in the statutory newspapers, (i.e., the London, Edinburgh or Belfast Gazette) as appropriate.

3.1.2 Liquidator — The liquidator of a company in a members' voluntary liquidation must be an authorized insolvency practitioner but, unlike in all other proceedings, he may be and often is from the company's auditors. The liquidator is selected by the directors of the company and appointed by the shareholders. Because it is presumed that the creditors will be paid in full they have no opportunity to vote on his appointment.

The liquidator's obligations are to:

(a) realize the company's assets;

(b) agree and pay the claims of creditors; and

(c) pay the surplus funds to the shareholders according to their respective entitlements.

3.1.3 Creditors' Position — A members' voluntary liquidation presupposes that all creditors will be paid in full. The liquidator is not obliged to advertise for

creditors' claims in newspapers. However, the liquidator must take reasonable steps to ensure that his appointment comes to the attention of any creditor and he may well believe it is appropriate to advertise for claims. This will particularly be the case if the liquidation follows on from the closure of a business. A liquidator may become personally liable to pay a creditor's claim if he distributes the assets without taking proper steps to establish and agree such claims.

Although the directors have to state that the company will be able to pay its debts within twelve months, it is common for members' voluntary liquidations to continue beyond that period, often because the liquidator is unable to obtain confirmation of the tax liabilities within this period. The liquidator will, however, not normally defer payments to creditors and their claims are usually paid when agreed.

Creditors now have a statutory right to claim interest at the 'official rate' on all debts outstanding in a voluntary liquidation for the period from the date of liquidation (or due date, if later) up to the date of payment.

If the liquidator is uncertain that there will be sufficient assets to pay all the liabilities in full, perhaps because of large provisional claims by the Inland Revenue, he may delay paying the other creditors in full until he has agreed all the liabilities. The claims of parent or other group companies are often voluntarily subordinated to those of other creditors to speed up the payment of outside creditors and avoid the interest penalty.

If the funds available to a liquidator are insufficient to enable him to pay the creditors' claims in full within twelve months, he is obliged to call a meeting of creditors and convert the liquidation into a creditors' voluntary liquidation. The liquidator need not resign or put his appointment up for confirmation by the creditors, but he may do so if he wishes. The meeting of creditors, however, has the power to replace the liquidator. He must resign if he was a member of the firm who were the company's auditors and should resign if there is any suggestion of malpractice in the previous conduct of the members' voluntary liquidation.

3.1.4 Shareholders' Position — When the assets have been realized, the creditors' claims have been paid in full, and the professional costs and liquidation expenses have been paid, the liquidator distributes the remaining funds to the shareholders. If there is more than one class of share, the distribution must be made in accordance with the rights of the respective classes, as set out in the company's articles of association (or constitution). The liquidator may be required to resolve disputes between parties claiming an interest in the company's shares.

The return of funds to the shareholders is made without deduction of tax, although a shareholder may be subject to capital gains tax on any released profit on his investment. Insofar as the liquidator will already have had to pay tax on any capital gain realized on the company's assets, there is here an element of double taxation.

The articles of association often permit the liquidator to distribute the assets of the company in specie (i.e., by transferring unrealized assets of the company directly to the shareholders). This is done only at the request of and with the agreement of the shareholders. If this course is desired (as it commonly is when the company is a wholly owned subsidiary of another), a resolution to that effect will be passed at the winding-up meeting.

Sometimes the liquidator is asked by the shareholders to distribute the assets (either in kind or in cash) before he has had the opportunity to establish to his own satisfaction that all liabilities have been paid in full. In this case, he will usually obtain indemnities from the shareholders to protect himself from the personal liability he might have to any unpaid creditor.

3.1.5 Termination of the Proceedings — When the surplus funds have been distributed, the liquidator convenes a final meeting of shareholders. Usually no shareholders attend this. At this meeting the liquidator will:

(a) present a summarized account of his receipts and payments for the approval of the shareholders; and

(b) put to the shareholders a resolution allowing the books and papers of the company to be destroyed after a certain period. Alternatively, the books and records can be returned to the shareholders. Because of the doubt whether any shareholder will attend the final meeting, a better practice is to include this resolution in the business of the initial winding-up meeting.

Copies of the liquidator's final account and formal statement as to the holding of the final meeting, and of the shareholders' resolution concerning the books and papers, must be filed with the Registrar of Companies.

The company will be dissolved automatically three months after the filing of these documents and the Registrar will remove it from the register. Apart from any responsibility for safeguarding the company's books and papers, the liquidator is discharged from his duties. In exceptional circumstances, the court has power to nullify the dissolution and restore the company to the register in a period of up to two years. Any property of the company coming to light after dissolution becomes Crown Property and can only be dealt with by a special application to Court. There is no automatic right of remedy in such circumstances and each case depends on the facts. It is thus important to ensure that all right and title to assets is properly dealt with prior to final dissolution.

3.2 Creditors' Voluntary Liquidation — A creditors' voluntary liquidation is a procedure for winding up an insolvent company, initiated by the directors and shareholders but subject to control by the creditors. It is the most efficient method of winding up an insolvent company, and the procedures are therefore adopted for the majority of liquidations.

3.2.1 Commencement of the Proceedings — If the directors become aware that the company is insolvent and they have no good reason to believe that it will regain its solvency, they should convene meetings of shareholders and creditors to put the company into voluntary liquidation and to appoint a liquidator. Failure to do so may result in their incurring personal liability for the company's debts (see §3.4).

The directors usually instruct an insolvency practitioner to convene the meeting of creditors and to address the meeting on behalf of the directors. The company's auditor may carry out this duty, but he may not accept appointment as liquidator of the company. It is usual for the practitioner so instructed to arrange for any monies received prior to the meeting of creditors to be banked in a separate trust account to be available to meet the costs of the meeting and essential company payments. The balance is paid to the liquidator on his appointment.

Several weeks usually elapse between the directors' decision to put the company into liquidation and the meetings of shareholders and creditors. During this time, the company will probably cease trading, especially if it is operating at a loss. If it can continue trading without obtaining further credit, it may do so to conclude existing contracts, and possibly to facilitate the disposal of the company's business as a whole.

3.2.2 Shareholders' Meeting

3.2.2 Shareholders' Meeting — The Shareholders must meet (often by proxy) to pass an extraordinary resolution that the company be wound up and that the person nominated by the directors be appointed liquidator; two or more liquidators may be appointed jointly if desired. The resolution requires a 75% majority. The shareholders' appointment of a liquidator may be overruled by the creditors, although if the creditors cannot agree as to who should act as liquidator, the shareholders' nomination will remain valid.

At least fourteen days' notice must be given of the meeting of shareholders. The company is in liquidation from the passing of the shareholders' resolution.

If it is considered that the company's assets may be at risk, and virtually all the shareholders are available, the shareholders may place the company into liquidation by waiving notice of their meeting. A liquidator may therefore be appointed quickly to take control of the assets and protect them, pending the creditors' meeting. He does not however have full powers of disposal, etc., during the period prior to the creditors' meeting.

3.2.3 Statement of Affairs — The directors of the company must make out a statement of the company's affairs, showing its assets and liabilities. Some or all of the directors must swear to the contents of the statement. It may be made up to a date not more than two weeks before the creditors' meeting. The directors must lay the statement before the creditors' meeting, and within seven days after that meeting the liquidator must send the statement to the Registrar of Companies.

3.2.4 Creditors' Meeting
(a) Calling the Meeting

A meeting is held to enable the creditors to consider nominating a liquidator other than the liquidator appointed by the shareholders, and to appoint a 'liquidation committee' (see §3.2.5).

The meeting must be advertised in the appropriate gazette and at least two local newspapers, and a notice must be sent to every known creditor. The meeting must be held within fourteen days of the shareholders' meeting and the notice will include either the name and address of the insolvency practitioner acting for the company who will furnish creditors with information about the company, or the address where a list of creditors' names and addresses can be inspected on the two days prior to the meeting.

(b) Proxy Forms

A printed proxy is enclosed with the notice of the meeting. Unless the creditor is a private individual or a sole trader who wishes to attend the meeting personally, it is essential that a proxy form be completed and lodged at the debtor company's registered office by the time stated in the notice (usually on the day before the creditors' meeting).

The proxy form appears straightforward, but in practice many are incorrectly completed and, as a consequence, the creditor is not permitted to vote. In any case of doubt, it is advisable for the creditor to seek professional assistance in the completion and lodging of the form.

If the creditor wishes to send a representative to the meeting to vote on the creditor's behalf, his name should be noted as the proxy-holder. If the creditor is uncertain as to which of several representatives will attend the meeting, alternative representatives may be named. Proxies should not be given in the name of 'the Official Receiver' or 'the liquidator.'

The creditor may state on the proxy form whether he wishes his representative to use his discretion and vote as he thinks fit, or whether the proxy-holder must vote according to the specific direction of the creditor, which must be clearly expressed on the form. In the latter case, the proxy enables the creditor to vote in a predetermined manner (e.g., for the appointment of a named person as liquidator).

The statutory wording of the proxy form encourages proxies to be given in favor of the chairman. As the chairman is invariably a director of the company, creditors may question his independence in selecting a liquidator, who must, among other things, investigate the directors' conduct of the company's affairs. Accountants or solicitors can attend the meeting of creditors as proxy-holders and vote on behalf of their clients.

Under Section 375 of the Companies Act 1985 a corporate creditor can give an authority under its seal (official signature) permitting a named individual to vote at meetings of creditors without a proxy but, in practice, this is not often done.

(c) Procedure at the meeting

The resolutions that can be passed at a creditors' meeting are for the nomination of the liquidator, the appointment of a liquidation committee and, where joint liquidators are appointed, the division of duties between them. There is no statutory procedure for a creditors' meeting, but that commonly adopted is as follows:

(i) The meeting is held in a public meeting room or at the offices of the insolvency practitioner convening it.

(ii) Creditors are given a statement of the company's assets and liabilities, as estimated by the directors, together with a list of the company's principal creditors and the amounts of their claims. The amount shown on this list does not prejudice a creditor's right to pursue his full claim if it is for a different amount.

(iii) The meeting is addressed by the convening insolvency practitioner, who will give a brief resume of the events leading to the company's failure. Although the creditors have no statutory right to ask questions, the directors will normally be prepared to answer questions put to them on matters concerning the liquidation and the financial position of the company. Skillful questioning can be extremely useful, and unsatisfactory answers may demonstrate a lack of good faith on the part of the directors.

(iv) After the questions, the creditors will have an opportunity to nominate a liquidator in place of the liquidator appointed at the shareholders' meeting. Any proxies for the appointment of named individuals are read to the meeting. Proxies in favor of the chairman are effectively in support of the shareholders' choice of liquidator, and these votes are frequently greater than those of the dissenting creditors present at the meeting. The creditors' resolution must be passed by a majority in value of those present (in person or by proxy) and voting. A creditors' nomination takes precedence over that of the shareholders, but if the creditors fail to pass a resolution the liquidator appointed by the shareholders will remain in office. There is a right of appeal within seven days if the shareholders and creditors reach different decisions, but in practice creditors who do not accept the results of the meeting usually petition for the compulsory winding up of the company as described in 3.3.

3.2.5 Liquidator — A liquidator in a creditors' voluntary liquidation must be an authorized insolvency practitioner and is commonly a professional accountant specializing in insolvency work. He is empowered to act from the date of the resolution appointing him. Certificates issued by the chairmen of the members' and creditors' meetings confirm his qualifications and his consent to act. His powers and duties are similar to those in a members' voluntary liquidation (see §3.1.2), although his remuneration is fixed by the liquidation committee or, if there is no committee, by the creditors as a whole.

The liquidator must publish his appointment in the same way as in a members' voluntary liquidation and must call annual meetings of creditors and shareholders until the liquidation is completed.

It is his duty to realize all company's assets, including those referred to in §3.3.5.

3.2.6 Liquidation Committee — At the creditors' meeting, the appointment of a 'liquidation committee' is considered. This is a supervisory committee whose powers commence when the liquidator issues a certificate of its constitution and whose duties include:

(a) fixing the liquidator's remuneration;

(b) sanctioning the payment of classes of creditors in full, or compromises with creditors;

(c) sanctioning compromises with shareholders or debtors;

(d) sanctioning the sale of the company's business for shares in another company; and

(e) deciding on the disposal of the company's books and papers.

In addition the committee usually authorizes the liquidator to employ solicitors and agents to sell major assets.

Creditors may appoint between three and five members of the committee by a resolution of a majority in value of creditors present (in person or by proxy) and voting. Although shareholders have the right to appoint up to five further members of the committee, they rarely do so. Moreover, the creditors can resolve to exclude particular appointees from the committee.

There is no obligation on the creditors to appoint a committee, and creditors are sometimes reluctant to be nominated. The duties of the committee are not onerous in most liquidations, and members of the committee can be of considerable assistance to the liquidator, not only because of their knowledge of the trade but also by authorizing actions for which the liquidator would otherwise have to convene meetings of creditors or apply to the court.

Members of the committee are not allowed to acquire the assets of the company, trade with the liquidator, or otherwise benefit from the liquidation (without the Court's permission).

3.2.7 Creditors' Position — The winding up of a company as a creditors' voluntary liquidation normally indicates that there are insufficient assets to pay all the creditors in full, or that the directors are unable to comply with the requirements regarding a declaration of solvency.

The appointment of a liquidator effectively stops actions by individual unsecured creditors against the assets of the company, because the liquidator can request the court to restrain creditors from enforcing judgments.

The claims of British and foreign creditors rank equally in law, except that no foreign taxes can be claimed at all in the liquidation of a British company.

Under various Limitations Acts, creditors' claims become time-barred after six years in respect of ordinary debts and after twelve years in the case of debts arising under certain legal documents. Personal injury claims are time-barred after three years. The period does not necessarily run from the date of contract and creditors should take legal advice before accepting that a claim has become time-barred. If a claim has not been time-barred by the commencement of the liquidation, it cannot be time-barred later.

Claims are agreed by reference to the amount due at the date of the resolution to wind the company up.

(a) Priority of Claims

The proceeds of the assets realized by the liquidator are applied in the following order:

    (i)   secured creditors, out of the proceeds of any fixed charge security (but not of a floating charge security);

    (ii) the liquidator's costs and remuneration;

    (iii) preferential unsecured creditors;

    (iv) creditors secured by a floating charge;

    (v)   unsecured creditors; and

    (vi) claims for postliquidation interest.

If, unexpectedly, any funds remain after all creditors are paid, these are distributed to shareholders as in a members' voluntary liquidation (see §3.1.4).

The position of each of the above classes is complex and is described in more detail in subparagraphs (b) to (g).

(b) Secured creditors Types of security and methods of enforcement are described in Chapter 4. A secured creditor may:

    (i)   retain his security and not take part in the liquidation proceedings;

    (ii) either realize or value his security, and claim for the balance not satisfied on the realization or valuation; or

    (iii) surrender his security and claim as an unsecured creditor.

If the security is not surrendered, the creditor still needs to be advised of the liquidation proceedings, to ensure the following:

    (A) He may act to protect and realize the asset constituting his security, by:

        (1) communicating with the company and the liquidator with details of the security;

        (2) insuring any tangible assets charged, unless he obtains confirmation that adequate insurance is continuing and that his interest as the secured creditor is noted in the policy;

        (3) taking possession of the assets or, if this is not possible, affixing a notice to them indicating that they are the property of a secured creditor; and

    (4) obtaining timely legal advice if the liquidator claims the assets, or requires the secured creditor to value his security, or the security is otherwise threatened.

  (B) He must not do anything to prejudice his security. In particular he must not:

    (1) return any assets, documents of security, or title deeds to the company or its liquidator, after the liquidation has commenced, except on legal advice; or

    (2) lodge any claim with the liquidator without giving details of the security held. Generally speaking, it is not necessary to value the security until the liquidator is in a position to make the first distribution (by which time the security will normally have been realized), although the liquidator has certain rights to require a valuation of the security.

To the extent to which the security is insufficient to discharge the secured creditor's claim, the balance ranks for dividend with the unsecured claims. Only security given by the company need be taken into account; third party security (such as a guarantee) need not be deducted in arriving at the amount of the creditor's claim.

(c) <u>Costs of winding up</u> Costs include:

  (i) taking possession of and realizing the company's assets;

  (ii) preparing the statement of affairs;

  (iii) convening the meeting of creditors;

  (iv) liquidator's expenses;

  (v) legal costs; and

  (vi) liquidator's remuneration.

(d) <u>Preferential unsecured creditors</u> Preferential creditors are as follows:

  (i) Value added tax (VAT) due and payable within the six months preceding the liquidation date, including any due by other members of a group, where such members have elected to deal with VAT on a group basis.

  (ii) Tax deducted from employees' wages and salaries under the Pay-As-You-Earn (PAYE) tax collection system within the twelve months preceding the liquidation date. The term 'employee' includes manual workers as well as clerical, technical, and managerial staff.

  (iii) National insurance (that is, social security) contributions for the twelve months preceding the liquidation date.

  (iv) Employees' wages and salaries in respect of the four months preceding the liquidation date, subject to a maximum of £800 per employee, plus any claim for accrued holiday remuneration. The Government may stand in the place of the employees in respect of any wages and salaries paid from state funds under the Employment Protection (Consolidation) Act 1978.

(v) Claims for money advanced to pay wages or salaries to the same extent to which the employees who have been paid would have been preferential under (iv) above if the money had not been so advanced.

(vi) Various miscellaneous taxes.

If there are insufficient funds to pay all the preferential creditors in full, they are paid pari passu.

(e) <u>Creditors secured by a floating charge</u> The nature of a floating charge is described in §4.7 and the receivership procedure is described in §2.4. The debenture-holder may be paid only out of the proceeds of the assets secured by the debenture after taking into account the cost of realizing the assets, the costs of winding up, and the claims of the preferential creditors.

Any surplus remaining after discharging the debenture-holder is available to the unsecured creditors.

(f) <u>Unsecured creditors</u> When all preferential creditors have been paid in full and the amounts due to any debenture-holders secured by a floating charge have also been paid, the remaining funds are distributed pari passu among the remaining unsecured creditors.

(g) <u>Claims for postliquidation interest</u> Interest that has accrued prior to the liquidation date on debts may be included in the claims of the creditors noted above. However, interest accruing after the date of liquidation ranks behind the unsecured creditors' claims.

(h) <u>Amount of claim</u> The amount of claim is subject to the following:

(i) The claim is for the contractual amount due, subject to any mitigating factors to reflect the actual loss suffered by the creditor.

(ii) If the claim is interest-bearing and secured, interest up to the date that the security is realized is normally paid in full, to the extent to which the security is adequate to cover the claim including interest. If the claim is interest-bearing but not secured, creditors may add the interest which accrued prior to the liquidation date to their claims, and make a further claim in respect of interest which has accrued since the date of liquidation. If before liquidation a creditor whose debt carries no contractual interest gives notice to the company that interest will be charged, it can be claimed at the lesser of the rate demanded and the rate payable under Section 17 of the Judgment Act 1938 (currently 15%). Postliquidation interest under subparagraph g is calculated on the greater of the Judgment Act rate and the contractual rate (if any), unless the contractual rate is found to be extortionate.

(iii) Claims in currencies other than sterling are converted into sterling at the rate of exchange quoted at the liquidation date.

(iv) Creditors may not include the legal costs incurred in pursuing their claims, except any judgment costs awarded before the liquidation date.

(j) <u>Method of claiming</u> Creditors' claims must be in writing to the liquidator. His address is given in the notice to claim, which is sent to all known creditors and advertised in the press. The notice to creditors will specify a limited period (usually one month) within which claims should be made. In addition, creditors may claim at any time until the final date shown in the notice of the liquidator's intention to make the final distribution, although they may not then be able to participate in interim distributions to the full if the funds remaining in the liquidator's hands do not permit this.

The liquidator will provide a form to enable the creditor to claim relief from value added tax on his debt. The form must be completed and sent to the liquidator, who will provide a written acknowledgment of receipt of the claim net of VAT. This acknowledgment does not signify the liquidator's acceptance of the claim.

(k) <u>Distribution to creditors</u> In a large or complex liquidation, the liquidator may only be able to realize the assets slowly, or he may be unable to agree all the claims. Under these circumstances he may make interim distributions to creditors.

The procedure for making distributions, whether interim or final, is as follows:

(i) the liquidator investigates all proofs of debt submitted to him and endeavors to agree all claims.

(ii) The liquidator sends a 'notice of intention to declare a dividend' to all known creditors who have not submitted a proof of debt. The notice will state the last date for submitting proofs of debt to the liquidator, not less than 21 days after the date of the notice, and that the dividend will be declared within four months of this last date.

(iii) Within four months from the date stated in the notice of intention, the liquidator must calculate and declare the distribution. He will then send the dividend and details of his conduct during the liquidation to the creditors. Arrangements can be made for the creditors to receive payment of the dividend by post or direct from the liquidator's office.

A creditor who does not submit his proof of debt in time to participate in an interim distribution is entitled to receive that or earlier distributions, provided that sufficient funds are available. If, however, the liquidator has distributed all the funds in his hands, the creditor has no recourse against the liquidator, even if the liquidator was aware of the creditor's claim.

3.2.8 Creditors' Rights to Information — The liquidator reports the progress of the winding up to the liquidation committee and also reports annually to meetings of creditors and of the company (shareholders). Although annual meetings should be held, these are not usually of great importance, and creditors need not normally attend unless they are dissatisfied with the progress of the liquidation. Most liquidators provide creditors, on request, with copies of the reports presented at these annual meetings, together with summaries of their receipts and payments.

Creditors may ask the liquidator at any time about the state of the proceedings and the prospect of dividends. Although the liquidator will usually be reluctant to give a firm estimate of the total dividend until the proceedings reach an advanced stage, he will generally give creditors such information as he can. If a creditor does not obtain satisfactory information from the liquidator, he can communicate with:

(a) the senior partner of the liquidator's firm, if the liquidator is a professional accountant;

(b) the liquidator's professional body, if any;

(c) the Insolvency Practitioners' Association, to which most (but not all) insolvency practitioners belong; or

(d) the Department of Trade and Industry (Insolvency Service).

3.2.9 Termination of the Proceedings — When all assets have been realized and all funds have been distributed, the liquidator must convene final meetings of shareholders and creditors. He must give at least one month's notice in the gazette of these meetings, which are normally held on the same day, and within a week after the meetings he must send a copy of his final receipts and payments account to the Registrar of Companies. Unless creditors are dissatisfied with the conduct or outcome of the liquidation, there is no need for them to attend the final creditors' meeting. The procedure for the dissolution of the company is virtually the same as for a members' voluntary liquidation (see §3.1.5).

3.3 Winding Up by the Court

The compulsory liquidation procedure is conducted under the control of the Department of Trade and Industry and the court and is therefore substantially more formal than voluntary liquidation. This mode of liquidation is particularly suitable if:

(a) the directors do not initiate insolvency proceedings;

(b) the creditors believe that there are matters that the official receiver, as an independent official should investigate, particularly concerning the directors' conduct of the company's affairs;

(c) the outside creditors are unable to agree with the directors as to who should act as liquidator but cannot force a nominee agreed between them on the company; or

(d) the assets are insufficient to pay a professional liquidator's fees.

3.3.1 Commencement of the Proceedings

(a) The Petition

The proceedings commence with the presentation of a petition for a court order for compulsory liquidation. A petition may be presented by a creditor, the company itself, or (infrequently) the Department of Trade and Industry where the liquidation is sought in the public interest. A shareholder can also present a petition, on the grounds of justice or equity, when no other alternative is available (for example in the case of a deadlocked dispute between shareholders). This rarely happens in practice. There are several grounds on which a petition can be presented, but the most important is that the company is unable to pay its debts. Inability to pay debts is defined as where:

(i) a creditor who is owed £750 or more has made a written demand for payment and the company has failed to pay within 21 days;

(ii) a judgment creditor has been unable to enforce the judgment against the company; or

(iii) it is proved that the company's liabilities, including its contingent and prospective liabilities, exceed its assets.

The procedure for presenting a petition to the court should be dealt with by the petitioner's solicitors. Creditors should bear in mind that it may be costly to wind up a company compulsorily, even if the petition is undefended. Although some of the legal costs may be recovered from the realizations in the liquidation, the directors' reluctance to put the company into voluntary liquidation may indicate that there are insufficient assets to meet such costs.

(b) Provisional Liquidators and Special Managers

At any time after the petition has been presented, the petitioning creditor may apply to the court for the appointment of the official receiver (in the case of an English company) or an insolvency practitioner as provisional liquidator until the petition can be heard by the court. The purpose of such an appointment is to protect the company's assets.

If the company is continuing to trade, the official receiver will normally apply to the court for the appointment of a special manager (frequently an insolvency practitioner), to manage the company and its business until the petition is heard. Such a special manager's powers are laid down by the court order appointing him. In practice, he often becomes the liquidator after the meeting of creditors.

Appointments of a provisional liquidator or special manager are comparatively rare and, in practice, are limited to larger companies. They are necessary on occasion mainly because a substantial period of time - often many weeks - can elapse between the presentation of the petition and the actual court hearing.

(c) Court Hearing and Winding-up Order

At the court hearing, the company may oppose the petition and present its own proposals for the payment of the debt (or set out the reasons why it considers that the debt is not due). Any creditor can appear at the hearing and be heard for or against the petition. Creditors are usually represented by counsel on such occasions.

In practice, however, most petitions are undefended, and in many cases the company is not even represented. If an order for the compulsory liquidation of the company ('winding-up order') is made, it has immediate effect; the company legally ceases to exist except for the purposes of winding up, the powers of the directors cease, and all employees are discharged.

(d) Official Receiver

On the making of a winding-up order, the official receiver ('OR') becomes the liquidator. The OR, who is an officer of the Department of Trade and Industry having the status of an officer of the court, conducts the preliminary stages of the liquidation. Within twelve weeks of his appointment he must decide whether to call meetings of creditors and members, although if he decides that it is not appropriate, the creditors can still require him to do so. If the OR calls a meeting of creditors, the creditors can elect a liquidator other than the OR. The OR also has powers to apply to the Secretary of State to appoint a private sector liquidator without calling meetings of members and creditors.

The OR remains responsible for investigating the company's affairs, even if another liquidator is appointed. The directors are required to attend the OR's office to provide details of the company and its assets.

The OR is required to report to the court whether, in his opinion, any matters in connection with the company's failure require further investigation. There is provision for the public examination of any director or other person connected with the management of the company if the explanations they give do not satisfy the OR or the liquidator.

There is no OR in Scotland. The corresponding duties are undertaken by the interim liquidator, or subsequently by the liquidator appointed by the creditors or the court.

(e) Statement of Affairs

The officers of the company must lodge a statement with the OR, detailing the company's assets and liabilities, within twenty-one days of his request. The OR has power to extend this period and, in practice, it is often several months before the statement of affairs is lodged. If the officers do not prepare the statement, they can be fined, although this is rare in practice.

The OR must send a summary of the statement to every known creditor, with brief comments on the company's failure. It is not necessary for creditors to take any action on the receipt of the statement, although they may be able to judge from it whether they should lodge formal claims, if they have not already done so. In practice, the statement of affairs, even if it is prepared several months after the winding-up order, reflects the directors' opinions of the value of the assets and liabilities and not those of the liquidator.

3.3.2 Creditors' Meeting (England and Wales only) — The purpose of the meeting is for the creditors to decide whether someone should be appointed liquidator in place of the OR, and to appoint a liquidation committee.

(a) Notices and Proxies

The OR will send a notice convening the meeting to every known creditor, together with a claim form (termed a 'proof of debt'; see §3.3.6c) and a proxy form. A creditor who wishes to vote at the meeting must lodge his proof of debt and proxy form within the time stated in the notice, unless he is a creditor in his own right attending the meeting personally.

The rules regarding proxy forms are similar to those in voluntary liquidations described in §3.2.3, except that a proxy in favor of the OR, who acts as chairman of the meeting of creditors, will normally be used in support of the nomination of the majority of creditors present at the meeting.

(b) Procedure at the Meeting

At the meeting, the OR gives a brief resume of the directors' explanations for the failure of the company and summarizes the company's assets and liabilities. He then asks creditors whether they wish to nominate a liquidator other than himself and will read any proxies received.

Two or more independent liquidators may be appointed to act jointly. If the creditors are unable to agree who should be liquidator, the OR will remain in office. An absolute majority of those present in person or by proxy at the meeting and entitled to vote is required for a nomination.

The meeting of creditors can also nominate a liquidation committee to act with the liquidator. When no such appointment is made, the Department of Trade and Industry will fulfill the committee's role.

3.3.3 Liquidator (England and Wales only) — In practice, if the company's assets are below £10,000, it is unlikely that it will be a commercial proposition for a professional liquidator, who is remunerated by a percentage of the assets, to accept the appointment. If, however, the assets are of a substantial value, or if it appears that any particular expertise is required in the realization of the assets, it is in the creditors' interests for a professional liquidator to be appointed, mainly because the considerable pressure on the OR's office limits his efficiency in difficult or time-consuming cases.

If the creditors resolve that a professional liquidator should be appointed in place of the OR, the OR will file the notice of the liquidator's appointment with the court, and the liquidator will then be empowered to act. The liquidator must be an authorized insolvency practitioner.

When a winding-up order is made either upon the discharge of an administrator or during a voluntary arrangement overseen by a supervisor, the administrator or supervisor may be appointed immediately as the liquidator of the company, without the OR's becoming involved at that stage (although he is still responsible for investigating the company's affairs).

3.3.4 Liquidation Committee — The description and role of the liquidation committee (see §3.2.5) also applies in a compulsory liquidation, subject to greater formality. This formality includes the requirements that the committee must sanction any litigation, or the carrying on by the liquidator of the company's business.

3.3.5 Assets Available to Creditors — The assets available to the creditors in a winding up by the court include all the company's assets at the commencement of the winding up, which is either the time of the presentation of the petition for the winding-up or, where a company was being voluntarily wound up before this, the time of the passing of the resolution to wind up the company voluntarily. Any bona fide transactions for value are protected, although payments made by the company after a petition has been presented may be recovered from any creditor who had notice of the petition.

Fixed and floating charges granted by a company within various periods specified in statutes may be invalid, and the liquidator must ascertain whether any of the charged assets can be released for the benefit of the creditors generally.

Assets that are available to the creditors may also include assets recoverable by the reversal of transactions at an undervalue and voidable preferences. The court may, on the application by the liquidator (or in the case of an administration, the administrator), make orders to reverse the effect of transactions at an undervalue entered into by the company within the two years before the liquidation (or the administration petition), unless the transaction was in good faith for the purpose of carrying on the business and there were reasonable grounds for believing the company would benefit.

Voidable preferences will also be set aside if they would improve the position of any creditor or guarantor in a liquidation, if the company was influenced by a desire to make such an improvement. This is presumed in the case of connected persons. The period is two years for persons connected with the company, or six months for those not so connected.

Such transactions will only be revised if the company was insolvent or was rendered insolvent by the transaction, but there will be a presumption of insolvency in the case of a transaction at an undervalue with a connected person. A preference frequently encountered is where shortly before liquidation the directors of a limited company discharge a bank borrowing that they have personally guaranteed.

The law of Scotland relating to gratuitous alienation is similar to that applying in England to transactions at an undervalue. The periods, however, are longer; five years for connected parties and two years for unconnected parties.

In Scotland preferences are called 'unfair preferences.' The period is in all cases six months. Either gratuitous alienations or unfair preferences are open to direct challenge by any creditor of a company in liquidation as well as by the liquidator.

If the company has at any time entered into a transaction at an undervalue with the intention of placing assets beyond the reach of creditors, the liquidator may apply to the Court for an order to restore the position to what it would otherwise have been. This does not apply to Scottish companies.

Funds may similarly be recovered for creditors by the reversal of extortionate credit transactions entered into by the company. Such reversals may include actual repayments or the surrender of security.

3.3.6 Creditors' Position — After the court order has been made, the unsecured creditors cannot take any action in respect of the debtor's assets without the court's permission.

(a) Priority of Claims

The rules concerning preferential creditors' claims are the same as in a creditors' voluntary winding-up (see §3.2.6a). In compulsory liquidations, the preferential claims frequently absorb all the funds available to creditors. Many compulsory liquidations are commenced on the petition of the Inland Revenue, Customs & Excise, or social security authorities, which may indicate that there are substantial preferential claims.

(b) Amount of Claim

The rules defining the amount of creditors' claims are in general the same as in creditors' voluntary liquidations (see 3.2.6h).

If the claim is submitted in a foreign currency, it will be converted by the liquidator at the rate of exchange prevailing at the date of the winding-up order.

(c) Method of Claiming

Every creditor wishing to claim in the liquidation must lodge a proof of debt form. This is a statutory claim form dispatched by the OR with the notice convening the meeting of creditors. Further copies of the form may be obtained from the OR's office.

The form should be completed with full details of the claim and sent to the OR or, if the claim is submitted after the meeting of creditors, to the liquidator. A secured creditor must provide details of his security on the proof of debt form, and, in any case of doubt, should take legal advice before submitting the form.

The liquidator will investigate the creditors' claim and admit (i.e., agree) the claim. If the liquidator cannot agree the whole or part of the claim, he will issue a formal notice of rejection of either the whole or part of the claim, giving the reasons for his rejection. The creditor must then apply to court within 21 days for an order reversing the liquidator's decision. This time limit will be extended by the court only in exceptional circumstances.

(d) Distributions to Creditors

Procedures for dividends on creditors' claims are identical to those in a creditors' voluntary liquidation. (See §3.2.7k.)

3.3.7 Termination of the Proceedings — When all the assets have been realized and the funds distributed to creditors, the liquidator will call a final meeting of creditors by sending them a notice and publishing it in the gazette. The liquidator will report to the meeting on the conduct of the liquidation and on a summary of his receipts and payments. The creditors may resolve to refuse the liquidator his release, in which case he must apply for release to the Secretary of State. If the creditors are dissatisfied with his administration of the case, they may take action against the liquidator under Section 212 of the Insolvency Act 1986.

Once the liquidator has vacated office, any other matters in the liquidation will be dealt with by the OR and the Department of Trade and Industry.

3.4 Liability of Third Parties — The third parties who are most likely to be liable for the debts of a company are the directors and shadow directors. Directors include all those who carry out the functions of directors, by whatever name they are called. Shadow directors are defined as those in accordance with whose directions or instructions the directors of a company are accustomed to act. There is a proviso that giving professional advice on which the directors act does not, of itself, make the adviser a shadow director. Shadow directors may include major shareholders who are not directors; bankers or other lenders who exercise control over a company by way of 'intensive care' operations; and parent companies, insofar as the boards of directors of their subsidiaries may be expected to obey them. Directors and others responsible for carrying on the company's business, including shadow directors, will not generally have any liability for debts contracted in the name of the company except in the following cases:

(a) Personal guarantees. Guarantees from directors are frequently requested by banks, and by hire-purchase and leasing companies, as a condition of granting credit facilities.

(b) Preincorporation contracts. Promoters are liable for debts contracted by them before the company was incorporated, unless a further similar contract is entered into by the company after its incorporation.

(c) Actions specified in the Insolvency Act 1986, including:

    (i)   wrongful trading,

    (ii) fraudulent trading,

    (iii) misfeasance or breach of trust, or

    (iv) trading under a prohibited name.

(i) <u>wrongful trading</u>

A director may be guilty of wrongful trading if he knew (or ought to have known) that insolvent liquidation of his company was unavoidable, and did not take every step that he should have done to minimize the loss to creditors.

The liquidator applies to the Court for a declaration that the director (or directors) be made liable to contribute to the assets of the company. The Court has complete discretion as regards a compensatory award to the liquidator, and can decide which directors have to pay and how much.

When the Court is considering the conduct of a director, it will not only look at the director's actual abilities but will also assume that he has the competence and expertise to be expected of a director fulfillling his role in the organization. As the tests of insolvency are inevitably finance-related, the finance director will be placed under a higher duty than his colleagues with other skills. The duty of the managing director or chief executive, because of his overall responsibility, will also be of the highest. A nonexecutive director may also be caught by the provisions, even though he may not be involved in the day-to-day running of the company. It will be assumed that such a director will have a monitoring role, resulting in a potential responsibility for the failure of the company. A shadow director, as defined above, can also be caught by the provisions.

(ii) fraudulent trading

Fraudulent trading may arise if directors or others knowingly cause the company to incur liabilities while it is insolvent, and have no reasonable expectation that the liabilities will ever be met. If it becomes apparent that a business has been carried on with the object of defrauding its creditors or anyone else, the liquidator may apply to the Court for a declaration that anyone who knowingly took part in the fraud may be declared liable to contribute to the company's assets.

This may catch a wider class of people than the directors or shadow directors affected by wrongful trading. However, fraudulent trading is also a criminal offence, and is rarely used as a means to recover funds due to the need, under criminal law, to prove intent to defraud beyond a reasonable doubt.

(iii) misfeasance or breach of trust

Any officer of the company, any person connected in setting it up or running it, any person who has acted as an insolvency practitioner in relation to it, who has diverted the company's assets to his own use, or who has failed in his fiduciary duty toward the company, may be ordered to compensate the company. Transactions that may be scrutinized in relation to these provisions include those in which contractual rights of one company are transferred, for less than full value (or no value at all), to another company controlled by a director (or shadow director) so that the profits are directed to the new company.

Application for a compensation order may be made by the Official Receiver, the liquidator, a creditor, or (with the leave of the court) any shareholder.

(iv) trading under a prohibited name

A director or shadow director of a company in the year before it went into insolvent liquidation may not trade within the five years thereafter under any name by which the company had been known at any time during that year, or under any similar name. There are a few exemptions to this provision, such as where the business has been sold by an insolvency practitioner.

Anyone who contravenes such a prohibition is personally responsible for the debts that the new company incurs during his involvement. The same applies to anyone acting or willing to act on his instructions.

This prohibition was introduced to reduce the incidence of 'phoenix companies' where a string of small companies was set up and each allowed to fail with the owner stripping out any profits or assets and moving on to the next.

(d) Actions specified in the Company Directors Disqualification Act 1986

The regulations of the Insolvency Act 1986 that make directors personally liable to the creditors for the debts of their company are supported by the Company Directors Disqualification Act 1986, which provides for the disqualification of directors and thereby protects the public at large by halting the careers of unfit directors.

Directors or shadow directors may be disqualified by the Court for up to 15 years from being a director of a company or from taking any part in the management of a company. If a disqualified person contravenes the Court order he is not only committing a criminal offence, but is also liable for any debts that company incurs while he is involved in its management. A similar liability falls upon any person who acts on the instructions of a disqualified person. Thus, a director may be personally liable for debts of a company which is not being wound up. He may become directly liable to individual creditors and such a liability will be joint and several with the company itself.

The most important category of disqualification order is where a person is shown to be unfit to be concerned in the management of a company. Other categories depend on more specific instances of misconduct (e.g., wrongful or fraudulent trading).

The court may consider a disqualification order either: against directors of a company that is solvent but that has been investigated under the Companies Act 1985 on behalf of the Department of Trade and Industry; or against directors of an insolvent company whose conduct has been reported upon to the Department by the insolvency practitioner acting for the company.

Directors of a solvent company may be considered unfit for matters including breach of duty, diversion of assets and persistent failure to fulfill statutory accounting and filing requirements. Directors of any insolvent company, past and present, may be considered unfit for the above matters and their responsibilities for:

— the insolvency of the company;

— any failure to supply a customer who has prepaid;

— any voidable transaction or preference;

— any breach of the requirements relating to the first meeting of creditors in a voluntary winding up; or

— any failure to comply with an obligation relating to a Statement of Affairs.

The Department of Trade and Industry requires insolvency practitioners to report on the conduct of directors of insolvent companies during the three years prior to the insolvency of the company. The Department must then apply to the Court for a disqualification order within two years of the insolvency.

The points noted above are the main cases in which directors and other officers of a company may be made liable for the debts of their company. In addition, they may be fined or imprisoned for committing any number of offenses laid down by statute. The penalties imposed in such cases do not form part of the assets available to a liquidator.

4. TYPES OF SECURITY AND ENFORCEMENT

In England, security can be created by contract, such as a mortgage, pledge, or charge, or arise by operation of law, such as a lien or attachment order. Liens may also be contractual.

The law in Scotland relating to security and enforcement differs significantly from that in England, and professional advice should be taken.

Details of security granted by a company over its assets, whether legal or equitable, must be recorded in the company's file maintained by the Registrar of Companies.

4.1 Land and Buildings

Any interest in land in the United Kingdom can be 'freehold' (in Scotland, 'heritable'), effectively meaning complete and unqualified; or 'leasehold,' where rights depend on the payment of a rent for a limited period of years (with or without a capital payment for the grant of the lease). All security involving land and buildings requires legal advice.

The Land Registration Act 1925 provides for the registration of title to land in England and Wales at the Land Registry, but even now not all land is so registered and the forms of security differ slightly.

(a) Registered Land

Land registered at the Land Registry and bearing an identifying number may be the subject of a registered charge. The charge is recorded by an entry, in the charges section of the Land Register for the property concerned, of the particulars of the charge and the name of the proprietor of the charge (i.e., the mortgagee). Subject to the terms of the mortgage agreement, the proprietor may, if the charge is enforceable, sell the land, or he may transfer the mortgage to a third party. The advantage of registered land is that the owner's title, once accepted, is guaranteed by the state.

(b) Unregistered Land

Title to unregistered land is evidenced by a series of documents known as 'title deeds.' The terms of a mortgage can be set out in a mortgage deed, which will deal with such matters as the method of repayment of the mortgage, the rate of interest, and the remedies of the mortgagee in the event of the mortgagor's default. The mortgagee's powers of sale are the same as in the case of registered land.

An 'equitable mortgage' (an informal but nevertheless effective arrangement) is normally effected by depositing the title deeds with the lender, but there must be an intention to create a mortgage; the mere handing over of title deeds is not sufficient. Equitable mortgages can be created without the deposit of deeds if the intention to create a mortgage is evidenced in writing.

This is, however, unusual, and the title deeds of the property secured are normally held by the first mortgagee, whether the charge is legal or equitable. It is normally necessary to obtain a court order to enforce equitable charges.

Any number of successive charges can be granted on a property.

Neither legal nor equitable first mortgages of unregistered land accompanied by the deposit of title deeds need necessarily be registered in the Land Charges Register, but mortgages in which the title deeds are not deposited with the mortgagee must be so registered.

(c) Position in Scotland

The position in Scotland is different, as security over land and buildings is governed by the Conveyancing and Feudal Reform (Scotland) Act 1970. All land and buildings in Scotland are registered in the names of their owners and the owner can grant a standard security (which is the equivalent of a fixed charge) over these assets as security against advances. A standard security must be registered with the Registrar of Companies and with the Register of Sasines to be effective.

4.2 Ships and Aircraft

Special rules apply to the registration of ships and aircraft and to any mortgages thereon. It is essential that specialist legal advice be obtained on any such matter.

4.3 Other Tangible Assets

Other tangible assets may be given as security by either mortgage or pledge. When the mortgagor remains in possession of the goods, the Bills of Sale Acts and the Companies Act 1985 apply whether or not the security is in writing, and complicated requirements regarding registration and terms must be complied with for the security to be effective. As a result, bills of sale are unpopular as a form of security.

A creditor may be able to enforce an effective lien against a liquidator or trustee for services provided in connection with goods in the creditor's possession, such as repairs, transport, or storage.

With the exception of debentures (see §4.7), other tangible assets are not often taken as security, although bankers and others can obtain effective security pending satisfactory conclusion of importers' transactions by holding documents of title.

4.4 Retention of Title

It is becoming increasingly common for suppliers to attempt to retain (reserve) title to goods supplied until they have been paid.

The retention of title conditions must form part of the original contract between the buyer and the seller and not merely appear on the invoice. Moreover, depending on the wording of the clause, the contract can amount to a form of security that is required to be registered. This involves practical difficulties and, although retention of title can be claimed in liquidation, receivership, and bankruptcy, recent case law has narrowed the scope for it to be effective.

4.5 Intangible Assets

These include insurance policies, stocks and shares, book debts and other rights. The Bills of Sale Acts do not apply to mortgages of such assets, and the normal way in which they are charged is by assignment to the creditor, with provision for reassignment on repayment.

Mortgages of shares are sometimes effected by the transfer of the shares to the mortgagee with an agreement for retransfer on the repayment of the capital sum. Alternatively, the mortgagor can deposit the share certificates with the mortgagee, together with either a memorandum of deposit in the latter's favor or a signed blank share transfer form and a deed of trust in the mortgagee's name. By these means, the mortgagor remains the holder of the shares in the register of the company concerned. Although a mortgagee's interest cannot be recorded in a company's share register, it is normal for the mortgagee to inform the company of the deposit of share certificates with him; this usually has the effect of preventing the registration and transfer of the shares without notification to the mortgagee.

Mortgages of debts are effected by either legal or equitable assignment. In a legal assignment, written notice of the assignment is given to the debtors, and the mortgagee is able to sue them without the cooperation of the mortgagor which, in the event of an enforcement of security, may be difficult to obtain. However, a legal assignment can relate only to past debts. In an equitable mortgage, the debtors are not given notice of the assignment and the assignee has no right to sue in his own name.

The factoring of commercial debts is of increasing importance as a method of financing trading companies.

Patents, copyrights, goodwill, partnership shares, and even interests in trust funds may also be mortgaged. Such mortgages are not common except where they are included under debentures issued by limited companies.

4.6 Personal Security

Personal guarantees are frequently required from directors or principal shareholders, particularly by bankers and major suppliers when the debtor company has not been trading for very long or has a low paid-in capital. This is because UK company law permits a nugatory paid-in capital for private companies. To be legally enforceable, a guarantee must be in writing and signed by the guarantor.

It is often advisable for a creditor to require a personal guarantee to be supported by formal security over the guarantor's assets. This is most frequently the guarantor's dwelling house, although the courts are sometimes reluctant to permit this security to be enforced when it involves a family house and the guarantor's spouse claims an interest in the property.

4.7 Debentures

A debenture is an acknowledgment of indebtedness by a limited company. It may be either a single debenture in favor of one lender (usually the company's banker) or a series of debentures or debenture stock which may be bought and sold in the same way as a company share. A debenture does not automatically grant security, although most debentures (strictly termed mortgage debentures or secured debentures) are worded so that they do, in fact, secure the indebtedness concerned.

When a series of debentures is issued, it is common for an institution to be appointed as trustee on behalf of the individual holders. The trustee can exercise all the powers of the debenture holders so that his position is similar to that of a single holder. Debentures are widely used to secure overdrafts and loans from companies' bankers.

(a) Form of Debentures

The debenture is a written document usually sealed (that is, officially signed) by the company creating it, containing an undertaking by that company to repay the sums due on a specified date or on demand. It also includes the following:

  (i) the name of the lender;

  (ii) the amount secured and a reference to the interest chargeable;

  (iii) details of the assets charged, specifying which are subject to a fixed and which to a floating charge;

  (iv) the lender's rights in the event of nonpayment of interest or capital, normally including the right to appoint a receiver; and

  (v) the rights of the receiver to manage and to act on behalf of the company under a power of attorney.

(b) Property Covered by Debentures

A company may charge any of its assets, including uncalled capital, goodwill, and future assets. The security given will either be a fixed charge or a floating charge. A fixed charge is a mortgage of specific assets and this is normally restricted to property such as land, book debts, and goodwill. A floating charge is a form of security which is said to 'float' over various categories of assets, such as machinery, equipment, or inventories, but it is not fixed because the company is allowed to deal with the assets concerned (e.g., by converting its raw material stocks into finished products for sale or to dispose of machinery due for renewal) without the problems of disposing of mortgaged assets; new or replacement assets obtained automatically become the subject of the floating charge. The holder of such a debenture is, therefore, able to maintain a charge over all the assets of the company while allowing the company to trade in the normal way.

If a receiver is appointed under the terms of a floating charge debenture (or on liquidation, or on the occurrence of any event specified in the debenture deed), the floating charge 'crystallizes' (i.e., becomes fixed), and all the individual assets covered by the floating charge form part of the security of the debenture-holder. The operation of a floating charge is sometimes difficult for a creditor to understand, especially if goods he has recently supplied are deemed to form part of the security of the debenture-holder, even though the supplier himself remains unpaid. A supplier incorporating valid retention-of-title terms in his contract of supply is entitled to recover his property even when there is a floating charge debenture.

(c) Scottish Practice

In Scotland the equivalent to a debenture is a floating charge. This is granted in favor of a lender (as in England, usually the company's banker) and covers generally all assets not covered by a standard security. There are some exceptions to this, such as goods which are covered by liens, hire purchase contracts and, in certain circumstances, goods covered by retention of title. The concept of a floating charge is a comparatively recent introduction into Scottish law, under statutes of 1961 and 1972.

5. DEBT COLLECTION PROCEDURES

Numerous procedures enable creditors to collect debts prior to the commencement of insolvency proceedings, although some of these are uneconomical and unwieldy in practice.

5.1 Commercial Practice

Prompt action is essential in matters of debt collection, and constant reviews of debtors' accounts, followed by regular applications for payment, are necessary. Even when this is done debtors can easily ignore written reminders for overdue accounts, although this is less likely if these are sent by the creditors' solicitors; letters from solicitors or reputable debt collection agencies frequently produce payments. Very often, telephone reminders are more effective in the collection of overdue accounts than statements sent by mail; an alternative to the telephone is the telex machine. During a period of cash shortage by a debtor, it is usually the creditors who exert the greatest pressure who are paid.

The ultimate sanction available to a creditor is to threaten to petition the court for a winding-up or bankruptcy order. Notice can be served requiring payment within 21 days, failing which an application will be made to the court for the appropriate proceedings. A court judgment need not be obtained before such a notice is sent. This course carries with it a slight risk that any monies recovered by the creditor after the presentation of the petition would have to be repaid.

The threat to commence winding-up proceedings is a powerful weapon, because a winding-up petition (although not a bankruptcy petition) must be advertised. This advertisement may adversely affect the debtor's business. Moreover, it is the practice of banks to close the debtor's account as soon as they are aware of the advertisement of a winding-up petition. For this reason, care should be taken not to commence winding-up proceedings for a debt capable of collection in some other way.

5.2 Legal Proceedings

Although any creditor has the right of personal access to the courts to take action against a debtor, creditors are strongly recommended to employ solicitors to avoid the risk that the proceedings might fail because the strict requirements of the courts have not been complied with. This is especially so in the High Court in London and the Court of Session in Edinburgh, where the closest attention to fine points of procedure is required.

Costs are sometimes awarded to creditors who are successful plaintiffs, but these are calculated on a court scale and are generally not sufficient to pay the solicitors' fees in full. Futhermore, the courts will not award any costs at all to creditors in actions for less than £100. A creditor must therefore decide whether an action for less than £100 is likely to succeed and whether any judgment obtained is likely to be paid, before he enters into expensive legal proceedings.

(a) English practice. Proceedings available to creditors in the collection of debts in England include the following:

    (i) <u>Judgments</u> A judgment is obtained by an issue of a 'writ of summons' and is an order of the court for the payment of a specific sum of money. It is important to bring the proceedings in the correct court. Proceedings for claims under £500 should be initiated in the County Court in the area of the defendant's address or registered office, or the area where the contract originated; if proceedings are commenced in the High Court and judgment is for less than £600, no costs will be awarded to the creditor; furthermore, if a claim for less than £2,000 is defended, any High Court proceedings will be automatically transferred to the County Court. In other cases, the advantage of taking action in the High Court is that higher costs may be awarded to a successful plaintiff than in the County Court. If the debtor does not defend the proceedings, the creditor is entitled to a summary judgment.

(ii) Writs of execution If a creditor is unable to obtain payment of a judgment order against a debtor who he believes has sufficient tangible assets to pay the debt, he can obtain from the court a 'writ of execution'. This is a court order to the sheriff or bailiffs (court officers) to seize and realize the debtor's assets. The writ will not be enforceable if the debtor immediately goes into liquidation or becomes bankrupt but, even if this happens, the creditor is unlikely to be in a worse position than if he had not obtained the writ. There is, of course, the risk that the debtor has, in fact, no assets available to be seized in this way, in which case the costs of applying for the writ will have to be borne by the creditor. These costs are not substantial.

(iii) Garnishee orders Bank balances and book debts can be attached by (i.e., diverted to) a creditor by the issue of a garnishee order. These orders, like writs of execution, can be applied for only after a judgment order is obtained. The effect of such an order is often avoided by the debtor, who can simply remove all funds from the bank account before the order is made.

(iv) Charging orders A creditor may be able to obtain a charging order (i.e., a mortgage created by the court) over the real estate (and certain other assets) of a debtor who is unable to discharge a judgment immediately, but who owns assets that are not already fully mortgaged.

(b) Scottish practice. In Scotland, the procedure for the collection of debts is broadly similar to that in England but there are some significant variations and the terminology is different. Legal procedures available include the following:

(i) Decree The Scottish equivalent of a judgment order is a decree. As in England, a writ is issued to bring proceedings in the Sheriff Court appropriate to the area in which the address or registered office of the debtor is situated. It is very rare for the Court of Session to be used for cases involving simple debt, as there is no monetary limit on the jurisdiction of the Sheriff Court.

(ii) Poinding and warrant sale. These are the equivalent procedures in Scotland to writs of execution; they are virtually identical in effect.

(iii) Arrestment. As with a garnishee order in England, bank balances and book debts can be diverted to a creditor by means of an 'arrestment', but the execution of an arrestment is significantly different.

First, an arrestment can be made at the time the writ is issued, when an application is made for an 'arrestment on the dependence of the action'. The funds in the hands of the third party at that time are arrested and cannot then be transmitted to the debtor. Secondly, even after decree has been granted, nothing happens until the pursuing creditor institutes an 'action of furthcoming' at the conclusion of which the arrested funds are transferred to the creditor.

(iv) Inhibition. As with an arrestment, an inhibition is a process that can be instituted at the time of issue of a writ. It relates only to heritable assets of the debtor (i.e., land or buildings owned by the debtor), and has the effect of preventing the sale of the asset concerned until the settlement of the debt.

6. SOURCES OF LAW

(a) Statute law. Company law in Great Britain is contained in a series of Companies Acts, in particular the Companies Act 1985. In Northern Ireland, the principal Act is the Companies Act 1960, which adopted many, but not all, of the requirements of Great Britain's Companies Act 1948. A short amending Act for Northern Ireland was passed in 1963. Since the suspension of the Northern Ireland parliament, company law in the province has been kept more or less in step with that in England by means of Orders in Council.

The insolvency laws relating to companies are contained in the Insolvency Act 1986, supplemented by statutory instruments such as the Insolvency Rules 1986 and the Insolvency (Scotland) Rules 1986; and other statutes, notably the Company Directors Disqualification Act 1986.

The insolvency laws relating to sole traders and individuals are contained in the Insolvency Act 1986, supplemented by the Insolvency Rules 1986, and the Deeds of Arrangement Act 1914. The law relating to the winding up of partnerships is contained in the Insolvent Partnership Order 1986.

In Scotland, these matters are dealt with in the Bankruptcy (Scotland) Act 1985.

Numerous statutes concern employment law; the most important from the insolvency viewpoint is the Employment Protection (Consolidation) Act 1978, as amended, which is primarily applicable in Great Britain.

(b) Case law. In addition to statute law, many fundamental principles of company and insolvency law are based on cases decided in the civil courts, many of which relate back to the nineteenth century. Copies of decided cases are fairly easy to obtain through major libraries or professional bodies. All civil courts are bound by the principle of legal precedent, and so are obliged to follow previous decisions of equivalent and higher courts. Cases decided in English courts may not necessarily be applicable in Scotland and vice versa.

Decided cases are identified by the initials of the law report in which they are contained and by page number and year.

7. SOURCES OF INFORMATION

(a) Registries. The office of the Registrar of Companies in England and Wales is situated at Crown Way, Maindy, Cardiff CF4 3UZ; a copy of the register is kept at Companies House, City Road, London EC1Y 1BB.

In Scotland the Registrar's address is 102 George Street, Edinburgh EH2 3DJ, and in Northern Ireland, 43 Chichester Street, Belfast BT1 4RJ.

Members of the public may inspect companies' files during normal business hours and obtain microfiche copies of the information recorded therein for a small fee.

The information kept on a company's file includes:

(i) copies of its constitution documents (memorandum and articles of association);

(ii) names, addresses, and other particulars of its directors and secretary;

(iii) the address of its registered office (i.e., its legal address);

(iv) details of all mortgages and charges over its assets; and

(v) annual return forms, containing lists of shareholders and copies of the company's financial statements.

Some real estate, and mortgages thereon, are recorded in the Land Register or (in Scotland) Register of Sasines (see §4.1).

There is no requirement in the United Kingdom that every business must join a chamber of commerce or be registered otherwise than as described above.

(b) Publications. Formal notices in winding-up and bankruptcy proceedings must be published in the London, Edinburgh or Belfast Gazettes, as appropriate, and some notices must also be placed in local newspapers.

Credit reference agencies publish weekly lists of judgment orders made against businesses, and details of appointments of receivers and liquidators. However, these are not necessarily exhaustive nor up-to-date.

Many trade publications carry details of proceedings against members of the trade concerned but these vary in quality.

(c) Other sources of information. Banks will reply to requests for information on the standing of their customers, provided that the request is made through a banker, in writing, and relates to specific and genuine transactions. Legal responsibility for such information is disclaimed.

All letterheads of every company must disclose the company's name, registered office, and Companies' Register number and location. Any company or individual carrying on a business under a name which is not its own must disclose the company's or proprietor's own name on all business documents and at each place of business.

If a partnership name does not consist of the names of all its partners, the name and business address of each partner must be stated on all partnership business documents and at each of its places of business. Partnerships with more than twenty partners need not list all the partners' names but must state where a list of all such names can be inspected.

UNITED STATES

United States
Table of Contents

UNITED STATES

NOTE ON LEGAL SYSTEMS AND PROCEDURES IN THE UNITED STATES

The United States consists of fifty states. Forty-nine of the states follow the common law, whereas Louisiana follows the civil law. In addition, there is the federal government, which is also on the common law system.

The federal government has the sole authority to deal with bankruptcy. Each of the states, however, has its own laws dealing with types of business entities, security for debts and the enforcement thereof, and debt collection procedures. Also, each of the states has its own peculiarities as to procedures other than bankruptcy for arranging the affairs of insolvent debtors or dissolving corporations (see §§2B, 3B and 3C). A discussion of each state is not within the purview of this chapter. Rather, the chapter will deal with those items that are true in most states based on uniform laws, model acts, similar statutes or case laws. Situations in which there may be variations will be so indicated. Creditors should seek local professional advice, especially when dealing with an insolvent debtor in a nonbankruptcy context.

1. TYPES OF BUSINESS ENTITIES

Business in the United States is conducted by sole proprietorships, partnerships (both general and limited), joint ventures, corporations, and miscellaneous other entities. Most major businesses are conducted by corporations, but many are conducted by partnerships and joint ventures. Corporations are governed by statutes adopted by each state, most of which are based upon the Model Business Corporation Act. These statutes have the same rules for small, privately-held corporations as they do for the largest public corporations.

In general, all entities may do business under an assumed name; that is, a name other than that of the sole proprietor, partnership, joint venture, or corporation. The only usual requirement is that a certificate be filed in a central office indicating the real name of the person or entity conducting the business under the assumed name. For corporations, this central office is usually with the Secretary of State; for sole proprietors and other entities, it may be with the Secretary of State or at a local office. Once the certificate is filed, the entity need not make any further reference to its real name in its business, with one important exception — a financing statement filed to perfect a security interest in personal property must show the real name of

1

the debtor, not the assumed name. Therefore, creditors should always check to determine the real names of their debtors.

1.1 Corporations

A corporation is a legal entity distinct from its shareholders. It can own property, and sue and be sued in its own name. In general, shareholders are only liable, in the event of the corporation's insolvency, for any unpaid portion of the subscription price of their stock. Shareholders may be liable for the corporation's debts, however, if the creditors can show that the corporation was the alter ego of the shareholder. Evidence of this might include failure of the corporation to follow proper procedures or intermingling of the corporation's assets with those of the shareholders. Also, shareholders who receive improper distributions from the corporation, such as dividends when the financial condition of the corporation would not allow them, are liable to repay those distributions. In addition, the shareholders in professional corporations are liable for their own malpractice and the malpractice by others under their direct supervision and control.

Corporations are bound by their Articles of Incorporation, which are filed with the state agency having jurisdiction over corporations, and by their Bylaws, which are internal governing rules adopted by the shareholders. State laws vary on mandatory and permissive inclusions in the Articles and Bylaws.

The name of the corporation must include 'Company,' 'Incorporated,' or 'Limited' or the abbreviations 'Co.,' 'Inc.,' or 'Ltd.' As mentioned above, however, corporations may usually do business under an assumed name, which may have no similarity to its real name and may not contain any of these words or abbreviations. Depending on the particular state, a professional corporation must have the words 'Professional Corporation' or the abbreviation 'P.C.' as part of its name.

All corporations may either be privately held or publicly owned. Corporations with 500 or more shareholders of stock in any class and more than $1 million of total assets must register with the Securities and Exchange Commission ('SEC'). Corporations whose securities are listed on a national securities exchange must also register with the SEC. Thereafter, they must file certain limited information with the SEC at the end of each of the first three quarters of their fiscal years and detailed information at the end of their fiscal years. They must also report to the SEC as certain significant events occur, such as acquisition or disposition of a significant amount of assets other than in the ordinary course of business and changes in control of the corporation.

Many states do not provide a minimum amount of capital. Typically, payment for shares may be made by transferring property or rendering services.

Corporations may usually pay dividends out of surplus, which is the excess of the net assets of the corporation over its stated capital. Net assets means the amount by which the total assets (valued either at book value or at current fair market value) exceed the total liabilities. However, a corporation may not pay dividends if, after paying the dividends, it is insolvent (i.e., unable to pay its debts as they become due in the usual course of its business). Corporations are usually authorized to redeem stock out of surplus if, after the redemption, the corporation would not be insolvent.

Corporations are usually managed by directors, but the Articles of Incorporation may provide that the power usually vested in directors will be exercised by the shareholders. The directors (shareholders) appoint the officers to handle the day-to-day business of the corporation. In doing business with a corporation, it is important to know whether the transaction requires the specific authorization of the Board of Directors.

1.2 Partnerships

A partnership is a legal entity distinct from its individual partners, which may own property and sue or be sued in its own name.

There are two types of partnerships: general and limited. In a general partnership all of the partners are *jointly and severally* liable for:

(a) damages caused by the wrongful act or omission of any partner acting in the ordinary course of business or with authority from the other partners, and

(b) money or property received by a partner acting within the scope of his apparent authority and misapplied, or property received by the partnership in the course of its business and misapplied.

In addition, the partners are *jointly* liable for all other debts of the partnership. All partners may bind the partnership for transactions apparently carrying on the partnership's business in the usual way unless the partner's act is, in fact, unauthorized and the person with whom the partner is dealing has knowledge of that fact.

The major differences between a general partnership and a limited partnership are that the limited partners are not liable for the debts of the partnership and the limited partners do not have authority to bind the partnership.

Partnerships must comprise at least two persons or entities, but there is no limitation on the maximum number. Partnerships are usually required to file certificates indicating the names and addresses of the partners. There is no requirement for a written agreement for the formation of a general partnership, but such written agreement usually exists. There is no requirement for an agreement as to a limited partnership, but the certificate filed by a limited partnership must contain many of the items an agreement would ordinarily contain. Although interests in partnerships may be transferable, unless restricted by the agreement, a transferee ordinarily acquires only the right to money otherwise payable to the transferor, without any of the power of the transferor to participate in the business of the partnership.

1.3 Joint Ventures

Except for those partnerships covered by SEC filing requirements, there are no requirements for filing of financial statements.

A joint venture is almost identical to a partnership, although it is formed for a single project. The only common difference is that in some states the authority of one joint venturer to bind the joint venture may be less than the authority of a partner to bind the partnership.

1.4 Sole Proprietorship

An individual owning and operating a business is referred to as a 'sole proprietor.' Other than the requirement of registering an assumed name, there are no requirements for central registration or filing of financial statements.

2. REORGANIZATIONS

The principal methods of business reorganizations in the United States are:

(1) Reorganization under the Bankruptcy Code (usually Chapter 11, but sometimes Chapter 12 for a family farmer or Chapter 13 for a wage earner), and

(2) Common law compositions or extensions, also known as out-of-court workouts.

Chapter 11 of the Bankruptcy Code and out-of-court workouts may be used no matter in what form the business is conducted. We will not discuss Chapter 12 or Chapter 13 of the Bankruptcy Code because the former applies only to family farmers, not the type of business covered by this book, and the latter only applies if the debtor is an individual with regular income with unsecured debts of less than $100,000 and secured debts of less than $350,000.

A. Chapter 11 of the Bankruptcy Code

Although there are several Chapters of the Bankruptcy Code of 1978 (Title 11 U.S.C. as amended) dealing with rehabilitation and restructuring of debts, Chapter 11 covers the reorganization of businesses, from a small 'mom and pop' store to the most pervasive reorganization of a major corporation with public and private debt.

The Bankruptcy Code is federal legislation, and the reorganization is monitored in the bankruptcy court under the supervision of a bankruptcy judge. The 1978 Act establishing the Bankruptcy Code also provided for a bankruptcy court with the most pervasive jurisdiction. While reorganization lawyers extolled the virtues of the expanded court, the Supreme Court of the United States struck down the pervasive jurisdiction as unconstitutional. Chaos reigned for a couple of years until Congress finally resolved the problem in 1984 with revised legislation on jurisdiction.

We mention the U.S. Trustee in many different sections of this Article. The U.S. Trustee system was established to remove from the court the administrative functions previously performed by the court. Originally established on a 'pilot' basis, it has recently been expanded to the entire country, subject to gradual phase-in, and the U.S. Trustee's powers have been more sharply defined. The most important duties of the U.S. Trustee are monitoring and commenting on fee applications, plans and disclosure statements, appointing the creditors' committee, trustee, and examiner, and monitoring the progress of cases to keep them moving. Keep in mind that the U.S. Trustee is different from the trustees appointed in all liquidations and some reorganizations. The U.S. Trustee is a government official overseeing all cases in his or her area. The trustee is appointed by this court to administer an individual case.

The new court system restricts the jurisdiction of the bankruptcy judges considerably, but it is the opinion of the authors that the activities of the judges will expand in the future by acquiescence of the higher federal courts supervising the process. Recent interpretation of the core jurisdiction by the higher courts seems to bear out this position.

2.1 Eligibility — Any person who resides in the United States or has a domicile, place of business, or property in the United States may be a debtor under Chapter 11, except the following:

* A domestic insurance company, bank, savings bank, cooperative bank, savings and loan association, building and loan association, homestead association, or credit union.
* A foreign business of the nature described above engaged in such business in the United States.

A person is defined to include an individual, partnership, or corporation.

2.2 Scheme of a Reorganization Proceeding — The general scheme of a reorganization proceeding is for the debtor or a third party to file a plan of reorganization. The plan may call for the composition of the debtor's debts (settlement for less than 100 cents on the dollar), an extension of time to pay, or a combination of both. The plan may impact secured obligations, unsecured debt, and equity interests. The plan may provide for the assumption, rejection, or assignment of any executory contract or unexpired lease, and it may also provide for the liquidation of all or substantially all of the assets, with a pro rata distribution of the proceeds among the various classes of debt and equity.

2.3 Filing — A reorganization case may be started in one of two ways: by the debtor's filing of a voluntary petition or by the filing of an involuntary petition by creditors. If the debtor has twelve or more creditors, at least three whose claims total more than $5,000 must join in the involuntary petition. If the total creditors are less than twelve, only one whose claim is at least $5,000 is required. If the debtor is a partnership, an involuntary petition may be filed by a general partner or, if all of the general partners are in bankruptcy, the trustee of a general partner or any creditor of the partners. The involuntary petition must allege and prove one of the two following grounds:

- General failure by debtor to pay its debts as they become due, not including such debts that are the subject of a bona fide dispute.

- The appointment of, or taking possession by, a custodian of substantially all the debtor's property within 120 days before the filing of the petition.

For the filing of a voluntary petition, there is no requirement that a debtor be insolvent. As a result, many major corporations with enormous net worth have filed Chapter 11 to alleviate special problems. Some examples are John Mansville Co.'s attempt to resolve present and potential asbestos tort litigation, and A. H. Robbins, which filed to resolve present and potential litigation arising out of injuries from the Dalkon Shield.

Upon the filing of a voluntary petition or the determination by the court that the petitioners have proved the grounds of an involuntary petition, the court enters an 'Order for Relief,' which orders that the bankruptcy case proceed.

2.4 Continuance of Business — The Bankruptcy Code authorizes the automatic continuance of the debtor's business once a petition has been filed. The business will ordinarily be operated by the debtor, which is referred to, during the pendency of the proceeding, as the debtor-in-possession. This is contrary to the approach under the prior bankruptcy act when the Court, which had the discretion to appoint either a receiver or debtor-in-possession, usually appointed receivers. The debtor-in-possession operates unless a trustee is appointed (See §2.7). The debtor-in-possession has all the rights and powers of a trustee and performs many of the functions of a trustee except those set forth in Section 1106(2), (3) and (4).

2.5 First Meeting of Creditors — Within a reasonable time after the filing of the petition and the entry of an order for relief under Chapter 11, an initial meeting of creditors takes place. The court is prohibited from presiding at or attending this meeting. The U.S. Trustee calls the meeting and presides over it. The meeting is usually perfunctory in nature, although this was probably not intended by the drafters of the Code. A representative of the debtor is required to appear and submit to examination under oath by the creditors. The examination usually relates to the financial history of the debtor, the reasons for its present financial problems, contemplated changes in the management and operation of the business, and possible preferential transfers and fraudulent conveyances.

2.6 Committees — The Code authorizes the appointment of an unsecured creditors' committee as soon as practicable after the order for relief by the U.S. Trustee, if there is one, otherwise by the Court. The timing of this appointment has varied around the country in both U.S. Trustee 'pilot districts' and nonpilot districts.

An equity security holders' committee may also be appointed.

a. The Code provides that the creditors' committee must ordinarily consist of the seven largest creditors who are willing to serve, but, as a practical matter, committees have varied in size from as few as three to as many as twenty-one in a major reorganization. A disturbing trend is the failure of creditors to agree to serve on committees even though their interests are impacted by the entire proceedings. There are no committees operating in more than 50% of the Chapter 11 cases filed in the country.

b. The creditors' committee may be changed as to membership or size after its initial appointment to ensure that it is a representative committee.

c. Additional committees of creditors or equity security holders can be appointed if a good reason for such appointment exists. Many such committees have been appointed with no uniformity around the country. Such committees have been appointed for retirees, tort claimants, labor representation, subordinated debt holders, etc.

d. The functions of a committee include consultation about the debtor's operation, investigation of the financial affairs of the debtor, participation in the formulation of a plan of reorganization, and the right to request the appointment of a trustee or examiner (§2.8) if it deems one necessary. A committee may also file a plan of its own design if the debtor's exclusive time expires (§2.13.1) or if a trustee is appointed (§2.7).

e. A committee has the power to select, with court approval, attorneys, accountants, and other agents as long as the selection is made at a scheduled committee meeting at which a majority of the members are present. Any professional selected by a committee cannot represent a creditor, if this representation would constitute the representation of an adverse interest.

f. All agents retained by a court-approved committee are paid by the debtor upon application and court approval. Sometimes there are informal committees that apply to the court for payment of professionals retained by them.

2.7 Trustee — A trustee may be appointed upon request of a party in interest or the U.S. Trustee. The trustee will then supplant the debtor-in-possession in the operation of the business, and the exclusive right of the debtor to file a plan will automatically terminate. The court may order the appointment of a trustee after notice and a hearing if cause is demonstrated, including fraud, dishonesty, or gross mismanagement by the debtor before or after commencement of the case. The appointment may also be ordered if it is in the interests of creditors and stockholders. This provision has been a catchall that the courts have used in several instances where they believed that a trustee was needed. Once ordered, the U.S. Trustee (or the court, if there is no U.S. Trustee) appoints the trustee.

2.7.1 — The trustee, once appointed, has several functions and duties in addition to carrying on the operation of the business.

- Perform some of the duties of a trustee in a liquidation under Chapter 7 of the Bankruptcy Code (§3), such as examining and objecting to proofs of claim, if necessary, and filing with the court, the U.S. Trustee and taxing agencies periodic reports on the operation of the business.

- Prepare and file schedules and a statement of affairs if the debtor has not already done so. The schedules list all of the creditors and assets of the debtor, whereas the statement of affairs answers various questions regarding the debtor's present status and recent history.

- Investigate all aspects of the financial condition of the debtor, the debtor's operations, and the desirability of continuing the debtor's business.

- Prepare and file a statement of the trustee's investigation with specific reference to fraud, dishonesty, incompetence, gross mismanagement, or to any causes of action available to the estate. This statement is to be transmitted to several parties, such as the creditors' committee, equity security holders' committee, and any indenture trustee.

- The trustee also has the right to file a plan of reorganization, but this does not eliminate the right of the debtor or other third party proponents to file a plan of reorganization.

   2.7.2 — In districts without a U.S. Trustee, the court appoints a person with operating expertise as the trustee, which person does not necessarily come from the panel of trustees maintained by the court for the Chapter 7 liquidation cases. The U.S. Trustee, when there is one, makes the appointment after consultation with parties in interest and subject to the approval of the bankruptcy court.

2.8 Examiner — In cases in which the court does not want to go so far as to appoint a trustee but still believes that an independent investigation of the debtor is necessary, the court may appoint an examiner. This position has no historical background in prior bankruptcy acts. The idea of an examiner crept in during the congressional debates as part of a compromise to appease the Securities and Exchange Commission, which wanted a trustee in every case involving a public company. Congress thought that the appointment of a trustee in every large case was unnecessary and would be an undue financial burden.

   2.8.1 — The provisions for the appointment of the Examiner are precisely the same as they are for the trustee. An examiner will be appointed when it is determined to be in the interests of creditors or equity security holders and is mandatory when the debtor s unsecured debts, other than for goods, services, taxes, and debts to an insider, exceed $5 million. The debtor often agrees to the appointment of an examiner to avoid the appointment of a trustee demanded by a party in interest. An examiner can accomplish almost everything that a trustee can except for actually operating the business and, as a practical matter, the powers of an examiner have been expanded by court order far beyond those contemplated by the drafters of the Bankruptcy Code. A reason that the debtor will often compromise and allow the appointment of an examiner is that the appointment of a trustee causes the debtor to lose the exclusive right to file a plan of reorganization, whereas the appointment of an examiner does not.

2.8.2 — An examiner has the following duties under the Code:

• Investigate any allegations of fraud, dishonesty, mismanagement, or irregularity in the management of the debtor's affairs by current or former management.

• Perform the duties assigned to a trustee in Section 1106(a)(3) and (4), such as the investigation of the financial condition of the debtor and desirability of the continuance of the debtor's business (see §2.7.1).

• File a report of this investigation with the bankruptcy court and transmit copies to the creditors' committee, equity security holders' committee, indenture trustee (§4.20), and others.

2.9 Administrative Powers — The debtor-in-possession or trustee is aided in the administration of the estate by the so-called Administrative Powers that are contained in Sections 361 through 366 of the Code. The drafters of the Code knew, however, that most bankruptcy judges were debtor oriented and did not properly protect secured creditors. The Code, therefore, adopted the concept that secured creditors must receive adequate protection of their interests in the debtor's assets; that is, the court must sufficiently protect the interests of the secured creditors so that they receive what they would have received but for the bankruptcy. This concept of adequate protection is derived from the Fifth Amendment protection of property interests from seizure without just compensation. Section 361 provides four alternative methods of providing this adequate protection of the secured creditors' interests. These methods are neither exclusive nor exhaustive. All of the methods, however, relate to the value of the protected party's interest in the property. The time and method of this valuation is not specified, and it was left to case-by-case development. Adequate protection can be given by way of cash payments, an additional or replacement lien, or other relief. Any entity granted adequate protection also receives under Section 507(b) of the Bankruptcy Code a claim that is prior to most other expenses of administration, if it subsequently develops that such protection was not, in fact, adequate. This claim is called a super priority claim and the only claims having a priority over it are the super, super priority claims discussed at §2.9.3.

2.9.1 — The first Administrative Power is the automatic stay, which stays the commencement or continuation of any litigation and provides the debtor with a breathing spell until it is able to formulate a Plan of Reorganization. Section 362(a) describes the various kinds of actions by creditors that are stayed, and Section 362(b) lists the five exceptions to the automatic stay, mainly government actions. If a creditor desires relief from the automatic stay, it can only be obtained by motion and a hearing. If a secured creditor seeks relief from the stay so as to foreclose, the concept of adequate protection comes into play, as well as the debtor's equity in the property and the necessity of the property to an effective reorganization.

2.9.2 — The use, sale, or lease of property, both in the ordinary course of business and out of the ordinary course of business, are covered by Section 363. This is the most frequently used of the Administrative Powers because of the many activities that it relates to during the operation of the business. One of the most important provisions in Section 363 is the prohibition against the use, sale, or lease of 'cash collateral' without court order, unless there is consent by all entities that have an interest in the cash collateral. 'Cash Collateral' is the cash proceeds of secured assets (for example, the cash collected from receivables or the proceeds from the sale of equipment or inventory). The debtor initiates the process by filing a motion for use of the cash collateral and must demonstrate that the adequate protection it will provide to the secured party will be sufficient. The battle on use of cash collateral usually takes place within the early stages of the case, and failure of the debtor-in-possession to obtain use of the cash collateral most often results in the demise of the company and conversion to a Chapter 7 liquidation.

2.9.3 — Section 364 of the Code covers the obtaining of both unsecured and secured credit and the incurring of debt both in and out of the ordinary course of business. All debts incurred during the course of administration in the ordinary course of business or with court approval are allowable as administrative expense claims under Section 503(b)(1). Subsection (c) of Section 364 authorizes the debtor-in-possession/trustee to grant a super, super priority to obtain credit or incur a debt, if it is unable to obtain unsecured credit by granting an ordinary administrative expense claim under Section 503(b)(1). This super, super priority granted under 364(c)(1) will be prior to any and all administrative expenses and also will be prior in time to the priority granted to an inadequately protected entity when adequate protection is involved. Because of this super, super priority most banks and lending institutions insist upon utilizing the features of Section 364(c)(1) rather than engaging in financing under the cash collateral provisions of Section 363. Section 364(c) also authorizes the granting of a lien on unencumbered property or a junior lien on encumbered property.

Section 364(d), on the other hand, authorizes the debtor-in-possession/trustee under certain circumstances to 'prime' existing liens by granting a senior lien to the new lender. A lienholder may only be primed after the providing of adequate notice and a hearing. At this hearing, the debtor-in-possession/trustee must prove to the court that the protection it will provide to the existing lienholder will be adequate. The money derived under this form of borrowing may be used in the debtor's general operation. Section 364(d) is rarely used because of the difficulty in proving adequate protection from a practical standpoint, but it has proved helpful on occasion when the debtor has an equity in the property and the lienholder refuses to engage in further financing.

2.9.4 — The debtor-in-possession/trustee has a right to assume or reject executory contracts and unexpired leases under Section 365 of the Code. An executory contract is a contract in which there remains something for both the debtor and the other party to do. This provision also authorizes the assignment of such leases and contracts under certain circumstances after they have been assumed. The assumption or rejection must be approved by the bankruptcy court. There is no definition of what types of contracts are executory, and the legislative history seems to indicate that it generally includes contracts on which performance remains due to some extent on both sides. The following are some of the interesting provisions in this section:

a. If the debtor-in-possession desires to assume, it must cure any default in the contract or lease and provide adequate assurance of future performance, if there has been a default.

b. No third party may be required to extend new credit to a debtor, whether in the form of loans, lease financing, or the purchase or discount of notes, without the consent of such third party.

c. There is no specified time period within which the debtor-in-possession must assume or reject an executory contract or a lease of personal property or residential real property. However, the nondebtor party to such lease or contract may file a motion to require the debtor to assume or reject it. The debtor may ask the bankruptcy court to exercise its discretion and extend the time within which this decision has to be made, if the debtor for practical reasons is unable to make a decision at that time. Where a lease of non-residential real estate is involved, the trustee must make a decision to assume or reject within 60 days of the entry of the order for relief in either a Chapter 7 or Chapter 11 case, unless the period of time to make such decision is extended by the bankruptcy court. The failure either to make such decision or to obtain a court extension results in the automatic rejection of the lease. It can be very costly to the debtor if this problem is overlooked during the chaos of the early administration of the case.

d. Clauses that automatically terminate a contract or lease, or permit the nondebtor party to terminate the contract or lease in the event of a bankruptcy are not enforceable under Section 365.

e. There are provisions giving lessors of shopping centers protection against a decline in percentage rents, a breach of agreements with other tenants, and a change of the tenant mix.

f. There are provisions protecting a lessee when its lessor files a bankruptcy proceeding and a land contract vendee when the land contract vendor files bankruptcy. In the former case, the tenant will not be deprived of its estate and will remain in possession under certain circumstances. In the latter case, the land contract vendee may either treat the contract as terminated or remain in possession, with the debtor being required to deliver title but being relieved of all other obligations to perform.

2.9.5 — Section 366 of the Code protects debtors from a cut off of service by a utility because of the filing of a bankruptcy case. The utility cannot refuse or discontinue service because of the nonpayment of a bill from before the bankruptcy, but the debtor must give the utility adequate assurance of payment for service provided after the date of the filing of the petition.

2.10 Property of Estate — The commencement of a bankruptcy case, whether under Chapter 7 or 11, creates an estate comprised of all legal and equitable interests of the debtor in property, wherever located, as of the commencement of the case. It includes all kinds of property, whether tangible or intangible, real or personal, all causes of action, and all other property recovered by the trustee.

a. Section 542 of the Bankruptcy Code requires the surrender of property belonging to the estate that is in the hands of third parties, and Section 543 covers the surrender of property by a custodian, such as a receiver, an assignee for benefit of creditors, and the like, who is holding the property in either a judicial or nonjudicial proceeding. When a custodian is involved, the court will provide protection for any obligations incurred by the custodian and for the payment of reasonable compensation.

2.11 Avoiding Powers — The Bankruptcy Code gives the trustee/debtor-in-possession certain avoiding powers to bring into the estate certain assets transferred before the filing of the bankruptcy. These powers are contained in Sections 544, 545, 547, and 553 of the Code.

a. Section 544(a), referred to as the 'strong arm clause,' gives the trustee the rights of a hypothetical lien creditor as of the filing date, both those of a simple contract creditor with a judicial lien and a creditor with a writ of execution. It also grants the trustee the rights of a hypothetical bona fide purchaser of real property of the debtor as of the filing date. Subsection (a) allows the trustee to look to applicable state law in his attempt to utilize the provisions of the strong arm clause. Subsection (b) gives the trustee the rights of actual unsecured creditors under applicable state law to void transfers.

b. Under Section 545, the trustee has the right to avoid the fixing of statutory liens that first become effective on the bankruptcy or insolvency of the debtor and liens that are not perfected or enforceable on the date of the petition against a bona fide purchaser.

c. Section 547 covers the avoiding of preferential transfers of money or property to creditors. It authorizes the trustee to avoid a transfer in which the following elements are met: the transfer was to or for the benefit of a creditor; the transfer was for or on account of an antecedent debt owed by the debtor before the transfer was made; the transfer was made when the debtor was insolvent; the transfer was made during the 90 days immediately preceding the commencement of the case or, if the transfer was to an insider, within one year; the transfer enabled the creditor to receive a greater percentage of its claim than it would receive under the distributive provisions of the Bankruptcy Code. There are exceptions to the trustee's avoiding power, and the creditor is protected if it can qualify under them. For the purposes of Section 547, the debtor is presumed to have been insolvent on and during the 90 days immediately preceding the filing of the petition.

d. Section 548 authorizes the trustee to avoid fraudulent conveyances by the debtor, if made within one year before the date of the filing of the bankruptcy petition. When the fraudulent conveyance was beyond the one year period and the applicable state law contains fraudulent conveyance provisions, the trustee may utilize the provisions of Section 544 of the Code. A fraudulent conveyance is a transfer of property or incurrence of debt

   (i)   with actual intent to hinder, delay, or defraud creditors, or

   (ii) with presumed intent because the debtor did not receive consideration reasonably equivalent to the value of the asset it transferred or the debt it incurred and

      (a) the debtor was insolvent after the transfer or debt was incurred,

      (b) the debtor's remaining assets were unreasonably small for its business, or

      (c) the debtor intended to, or believed it would incur debts it could not repay in a timely fashion.

e. Section 549 authorizes the trustee to avoid unauthorized transfers of property that occur after the commencement of the case.

f. Section 553 allows the trustee to avoid the setting-off by a creditor of a debt owed by it to the debtor against a claim of the creditor against the debtor if

   (i)   the creditor's claim is disallowed,

   (ii) the creditor acquired the claim during the 90 days preceding the case while the debtor was insolvent,

   (iii) the debt being set off was incurred for the purpose of obtaining a right of setoff while the debtor was insolvent and during the 90-day prebankruptcy period, or

   (iv) the creditor improved its position in the 90-day period.

   Otherwise, the Code recognizes the right of a creditor to set off mutual debts.

g. The avoiding powers of the trustee are subject to certain exceptions under Section 546, including the right of a seller of goods on credit to get them back if the buyer received them while insolvent and the seller demands their return in writing within ten days after the debtor received them.

2.12 Proofs of Claim — It is not necessary for a creditor or an equity security holder to file a proof of claim or interest in a reorganization case if the claim or interest appears in the schedules filed by the debtor, because the claim or interest is deemed filed. If the claim or interest is scheduled, however, as disputed, contingent or unliquidated or if the debtor neglects to schedule the claim or interest, it is necessary to file a proof of claim or interest. A cautious creditor should always file a proof of claim.

2.12.1 — The local rules usually cover the setting of a cutoff date for the filing of proofs of claims or interests when they are scheduled as disputed, contingent or unliquidated or they are not scheduled at all.

2.12.2 — Section 507 describes claims entitled to priority in distribution, and they are as follows:

- Administrative expenses allowed under Section 503(b).
- Unsecured claims incurred in the gap between the filing of an involuntary petition and the granting of the Order for Relief.
- Unsecured claims for wages, salaries, or commissions earned by an individual within 90 days before the filing date or the date of the cessation of the debtor's business, whichever occurs first, but not to exceed $2,000 for each individual.
- Unsecured claims for contributions to an employee benefit plan arising from services rendered within 180 days before the filing date or the date of the cessation of the debtor's business, whichever occurs first, but again with certain limitations set forth in the Code.
- Unsecured claims of persons engaged in the production or raising of grain or engaged as a United States fisherman.
- Deposit claims to the extent of $900 for each individual, if the money was deposited in connection with the purchase, lease, or rental of property, or the purchase of services for the personal, family, or household use of such individual.
- Various kinds of taxes of governmental units subject to certain limitations.

2.12.3 — If an entity is liable on or has secured a claim against the debtor, Section 509 provides when the entity is subrogated to the claim of the creditor and when the claim of the entity is subordinated to the claim of the creditor.

2.12.4 — Section 510 of the Code deals with the subordination of claims and recognizes the duty of the court to enforce subordination agreements. It also permits the court to subordinate on equitable grounds all or any part of an allowed claim or interest to all or any part of another allowed claim or interest.

2.12.5 — The determination of the secured status of a creditor is dealt with in a special section of the Code, Section 506. If the secured creditors' collateral is worth less than the secured debt, the section separates the claim into two parts: a secured claim to the extent of the value of the collateral and an unsecured claim for the balance of the claim. There is no indication of the type of valuation contemplated, it being left to the courts on a case-by-case basis, taking into account the facts of each case and the competing interests in the case. The determination of value for one purpose is not binding upon the parties for other purposes, but a secured creditor must be extremely cautious in the early stages of a case. For instance, the secured creditor might attempt to show a low value of the collateral in the early stages of the case in an attempt to lift the automatic stay, but this low valuation might come back to haunt the secured creditor at the plan stage when the secured creditors' claim might be valued for purposes of a 'cramdown' (see §2.13.11).

An oversecured creditor is entitled to interest and attorney fees during the pendence of the proceeding, but some courts have even allowed interest to an undersecured creditor as 'lost opportunity cost', computed on the value of the collateral. The issue of 'lost opportunity cost' is now before the United States Supreme Court because of a difference of opinion between various Courts of Appeal. A secured creditor's property may also be subjected to the reasonable, necessary costs and expenses of preserving and disposing of such property to the extent of any benefit to the secured creditor. This provision has been extended by bankruptcy courts far beyond the preservation theories originally contemplated by Congress at the time of the passage of the provision.

2.13 Plan of Reorganization — When the debtor has stabilized its operations and raised the necessary money to fund a plan, then and only then can the debtor proceed to the plan stage, unless the debtor proposes to sell its assets and distribute the proceeds. If the debtor no longer has the exclusive right to file a plan, however, a third party proponent could proceed to a plan before the debtor is ready.

2.13.1 — The debtor has the exclusive right to file a plan of reorganization for 120 days after the entry of the order for relief under Chapter 11. If the plan is filed within the 120-day period, the exclusive right continues to allow the debtor to gain acceptance of the plan before the expiration of 180 days after the order for relief. A party in interest, including a trustee, a creditors' committee, an equity security holders' committee, a creditor, etc., (called the proponent of a plan) may file a plan only under the following conditions;

- A trustee has been appointed;
- The debtor has not filed the plan within 120 days after the order for relief and has lost exclusivity; or
- The debtor has filed a plan in a timely fashion, but not obtained its acceptance within 180 days after the order for relief.

The court may, for cause, reduce or increase the 120- and 180-day periods upon request of a party in interest. Usually an extension is for a relatively short period of time, and the debtor may seek a further extension.

2.13.2 — The Code provides for certain mandatory and permissive provisions in a plan of reorganization. If the plan is a debtor's plan, the contents of the plan are usually determined by negotiations between the debtor, secured creditors, and the various committees.

2.13.3 — One of the first things to be considered is the classification of claims and interests. A class may contain only substantially similar claims or interests, but the Code does not prevent the classifying of such claims or interests in separate classes. The cases seem to indicate that the separation of similar claims into different classes must be reasonable and necessary and not discriminate. An unsecured creditor cannot be placed in a class with a secured creditor, a real estate mortgagee cannot be put in the same class with a creditor whose claim is secured by personal property, and a first mortgagee and second mortgagee on the same property cannot be properly classified together. The Code permits the plan to contain a separate class of small unsecured creditors, if the court deems the provision reasonable and necessary for administrative convenience. Where to draw the line for administrative convenience is a practical problem, decided by the courts on a case-by-case basis.

2.13.4 — A plan must do the following:

- Designate the classes of claims and interests.
- Specify the classes of claims or interests that are unimpaired.
- Indicate the treatment of any classes of claims or interests impaired under the plan.
- Provide the same treatment for each claim or interest of a particular class, unless a holder agrees to take less.
- Provide adequate means for the plan's implementation.
- Prohibit the issuance of nonvoting equity securities and provide for an appropriate distribution of voting power.
- Contain only provisions that are consistent with the interests of creditors and equity security holders and with public policy with respect to the selection of officers, directors, and trustees and their successors.

2.13.5 — A plan may:

- Impair or leave unimpaired any class of secured or unsecured claims, or class of interests.
- Provide for the rejection, assumption, or assignment of any executory contract or unexpired lease not previously rejected during the course of the proceeding.
- Settle or adjust any claims or interests of the debtor or provide for their retention and enforcement after confirmation.
- Provide for a plan of liquidation by the sale of all or substantially all of the debtor's property.

• Contain any other appropriate provision not inconsistent with the Code.

2.13.6 — If the plan of reorganization relates to the assets of an individual debtor, and the plan is proposed by a third party proponent without the debtor's consent, the assets of an individual debtor that are exempt by Section 522 cannot be used, sold, or leased.

2.13.7 — Section 1124 of the Code discusses the concept of impairment as materially affecting the contractual rights of creditors or interest holders. The acceptance of a class of creditors or interests whose claims are unimpaired is not required for acceptance of the plan of reorganization. Therefore, the concept of impairment is very closely tied to the confirmation standards and the cramdown under Section 1129(b) (for the confirmation standards see §2.13.10 b; for the cramdown see §2.13.11).

2.13.8 — The Disclosure Process

a. Prior to the solicitation of acceptances for a plan of reorganization, the plan proponent must first follow the disclosure process set forth in Section 1125 of the Code. This involves the preparation of a disclosure statement which must be approved by the bankruptcy court at a disclosure hearing prior to the distribution of the plan and the disclosure statement to creditors. The statement must contain adequate information, which is a substantive standard being developed on a case-by-case basis. The disclosure statement contains information relating to the history of the debtor and the reasons for its financial demise. It also contains a description of the provisions of the plan of reorganization, and a description of the tax consequences of the plan. The disclosure statement does not have to be as extensive as a prospectus used for a new issue of securities.

b. The legislative history indicates that the disclosure hearing is to be one of the most important hearings in the entire reorganization process.

c. The Code contains an extremely important 'Safe Harbour' provision that protects any person who solicits in good faith and in compliance with the Code from liability for violation of any federal or state securities laws.

2.13.9 — Acceptance of the Plan

a. Assuming that the Disclosure Statement has been approved, a copy of the Disclosure Statement, plan of reorganization, and a ballot are forwarded to creditors and equity security holders.

b. A class of creditors has accepted a plan when two-thirds in amount and more than one-half in number of the voting members of the class accept the plan. A class of interests has accepted when two-thirds in amount of the interests of the voting members of the class accept the plan.

c. Holders of claims or interest must actually vote to accept or reject the plan to

c. Holders of claims or interest must actually vote to accept or reject the plan to be included in the computation.

d. A class that is not impaired is conclusively presumed to have accepted the plan. A class that is to receive nothing under the plan is deemed to have rejected the plan.

***2.13.10* —** Confirmation.

a. The plan of reorganization does not become effective until it is confirmed by the court at a confirmation hearing. At the hearing the court applies the confirmation standards set forth in Sections 1129(a) and (b). If the proponent of the plan does not meet these standards, the Court cannot confirm the plan.

b. The court must confirm a plan of reorganization if all of the following standards as set forth in 1129(a) are met:

- The plan complies with the applicable provisions of Title 11.

- The proponent of the plan complies with the applicable provisions of Title 11.

- The plan was proposed in good faith and not by any means forbidden by law.

- Any payments made or to be made for fees and for costs and expenses in connection with the case and the plan are disclosed to the court and approved as reasonable.

- The proponent of the plan has disclosed the identity and affiliations of any person who will serve as a director or officer after confirmation, and the appointment is consistent with the interests of creditors and equity security holders, and with public policy. In addition, the proponent has disclosed the identity of any insider who will be employed or retained and the nature of the compensation.

- Any governmental regulatory commission having jurisdiction over the rate structure of the Debtor has approved any rate change provided for in the plan, or the rate change is conditioned on such approval.

- Each holder of a claim or interest in an impaired class has accepted the plan or will receive property, as of the effective date of the plan, of a value not less than it would receive in a liquidation. This is known as the 'best interests of creditors' test.

- Each class of claims or interests has either accepted the plan or is not impaired under the plan. Even if the class has accepted the plan, it must still comply with the 'best interest of creditors' test, which protects the minority members of a class. If an impaired class does not accept the plan, the fair and equitable test of §1129(b), including its cramdown provisions, will come into play (for the cramdown provisions see §2.13.11). Before this can happen, at least one impaired class must accept the plan.

- The plan provides for the payment of allowed administrative expense claims and 'gap' claims entitled to priority under Section 507(a)(1) and (2) in cash on the effective date of the plan. Gap claims are the claims incurred between the filing of an involuntary petition and the entry of the order for relief.

  (1) Wage, fringe benefit, and consumer deposit claims entitled to priority may be classified. A plan may then offer any of such classes deferred cash payments of a value, as of the effective date of the plan, equal to the allowed amount of such claim. If the class does not accept, it must receive cash on the effective date of the plan.

  (2) The plan may require priority tax claimants to take deferred cash payments over a period not to exceed six years from the date of the assessment of the tax without the consent of the taxing agency. The payments must include interest so that the value of the deferred payments will equal the allowed amount of the claim on the effective date of the plan.

- If a class of claims is impaired under the plan, at least one impaired class of claims has accepted the plan. The claims of insiders are not to be included in computing the number and amount of acceptances.

- Confirmation is not likely to be followed by a liquidation unless such liquidation is proposed in the plan. This is the so-called 'feasibility' test.

2.13.11 *The Fair and Equitable Rule* — Also known as 'Cramdown'

a. The Court must confirm a plan even though it is not accepted by all impaired classes of claims or interests if all the other requirements of Section 1129(a) are met and if:

- The plan does not 'discriminate unfairly'; and
- The plan is 'fair and equitable' with respect to each class of claims that is impaired and has not accepted the plan.

b. The proponent of the plan must request the application of the cramdown provisions.

c. The term 'discriminate unfairly' is a term of art nowhere defined in the Code, having its primary application in cases in which there is a class of subordinated debt.

d. Section 1129(b)(2) sets forth the 'fair and equitable' requirements for classes of secured claims, unsecured claims, and interests. The Cramdown is a sort of modified absolute priority rule, which requires that each class in descending order receive its full value before any lower class could participate in a plan of reorganization. Congress introduced the modified absolute priority rule to allow negotiations between classes of claims and interests. Therefore, if higher classes on the ladder agree to allow a lower class to participate without the higher classes' receiving payment in full, it is allowed under Section 1129(b). If the plan is not consensual, it must strictly adhere to the priorities set forth in Section 1129(b).

e. Although the cramdown standards are pretty clear, three courts of appeal have now recognized the right of equity participation even if creditors have not been paid in full where the equity holders make a 'substantial contribution.'

f. With respect to a class of secured claims, the plan is fair and equitable if:

(1) The holders of such claims retain their liens on the collateral, to the extent of the allowed amount of their claims, whether the collateral is retained by the debtor or transferred to another entity; and each holder receives deferred cash payments totalling at least the allowed amount of such claim with a present value equal to the value of the collateral.

(a) 'Allowed secured claim' means the value of the collateral unless the class elects to have the entire allowed amount of the debt relating to the property be secured by the lien even if the value of the collateral is less than the amount of the debt. In that case, the class gives up its unsecured claim for the excess of the debt over the value;

(2) The plan provides for the sale of the property, subject to Section 363(k), free and clear of liens, with the liens to attach to the proceeds, and liens on the proceeds of the sale to be treated in accordance with paragraph 1 above or the following paragraph 3; or

(3) The plan provides for the realization by such holders of the 'indubitable equivalent' of such claims.

g. A plan is fair and equitable as to a class of unsecured claims if:

(1) The plan provides that such claims will receive property with a present value equal to the allowed amount of their claims; or

(2) The plan provides that no class junior to the nonaccepting class will receive any property under the plan.

h. A plan is fair and equitable as to a class of interests if:

(1) The plan provides that the holders of the interests receive property of a present value equal to the greatest of any fixed liquidation preference, any fixed redemption price to which the holder is entitled, and the value of the interest; or

(2) The plan provides that holders of junior interests will not receive any property under the plan.

2.13.12 — The court may confirm only one plan. If more than one plan meets the requirements of Section 1129, the court considers the preference of creditors and equity security holders in determining which plan to confirm.

2.13.13 — The court may not confirm a plan if the principal purpose of the plan is the avoidance of taxes or the avoidance of Section 5 of the Securities Act of 1933.

2.14 Effects of Confirmation

a. The provisions of a confirmed plan bind the debtor, all creditors, and all equity security holders or general partners of the debtor.

b. Confirmation of a plan vests in the debtor all the property of the estate.

c. Upon confirmation of a plan, the property dealt with by the plan is free and clear of all claims and interests except as provided in subsections (d)(2) and (d)(3) of Section 1141(c), in the plan, or in the order of confirmation.

d. The confirmation of a plan discharges a debtor from all its debts existing at the time of filing the Chapter 11 petition and all debts that arose after the filing of the case and before confirmation. However, it does not discharge an individual debtor from any debt excepted from discharge under Section 523. In addition, confirmation does not discharge a debtor if the confirmed plan is a liquidating plan, the debtor does not engage in business after consummation of the plan, and the debtor would be denied a discharge under Section 727(a) if the case were a Chapter 7 case (for exceptions from discharge under Chapter 7, see further §3.11). Thus, in a nonliquidating plan of a corporation, all debts of the corporation, including fraud debts, are discharged. The confirmation of a plan also terminates the rights and interests of equity security holders and general partners who are provided for in the plan.

2.15 Revocation of Order of Confirmation — At any time before 180 days after the entry of the order of confirmation, the court may revoke the order of confirmation, if the order was procured by fraud.

2.16 Aircraft and Vessels — Chapter 11 contains special provisions in Section 1110 regarding aircraft equipment and vessels.

2.17 Railroads — There is also a special subchapter of Chapter 11 that relates to railroad reorganizations. Much of the provisions of Chapter 11 are applicable to this subchapter except seven sections specifically referred to as not applying.

B. Common Law Compositions or Extensions (out-of-court workouts)

2.18 Basis — Restructuring of debt in a Chapter 11 proceeding can be expensive and time consuming. Many debtors, therefore, prefer the out-of-court route involving either a composition or extension, or a combination of both. This remedy has no statutory basis, its origin being the common law.

2.19 Types — A composition involves a settlement of debt for less than 100 cents on the dollar, whereas an extension involves a payment over a deferred period of time. The debtor in a composition might offer a straight cash settlement or a partial cash down payment with the balance of the settlement amount paid over a period of time.

2.20 Availability — This remedy may be utilized by a corporation, partnership, or individual. The composition or extension cannot bind nonassenting creditors and, therefore, requires the consent of at least 90% in amount of the outstanding claims from a practical standpoint to be effective. This is a general rule of thumb around the country, but the agreement between the debtor and the creditors' committee often allows either or both to reduce the percentage, depending on circumstances.

2.21 Procedure — The process is usually started by the debtor's convening a meeting of 15 or 20 of its largest creditors, although an isolated few have been commenced by a letter from the debtor addressed to its major creditors. The latter form is very ineffective and usually results in the major creditors' insisting upon a meeting before they will indicate acceptance. Credibility is lent to the entire proceeding if the offices of a major trade or credit organization are used as the host for such meeting. An example is the National Association of Credit Management with offices in various parts of the country.

2.21.1 — The debtor describes the reasons for its financial difficulties at this meeting, hands out financial information, and undoubtedly asks for a moratorium or freeze on the payment of its debts for at least 60 to 90 days until it is able to devise a plan satisfactory to creditors.

2.21.2 — Creditors then resolve themselves into a committee, if they are not interested in a bankruptcy proceeding, and usually those creditors present who want to serve become the committee. The committee selects counsel and accountants to represent it during the period of the workout, and these professionals are paid by the debtor.

2.21.3 — If the committee and debtor agree upon an appropriate moratorium period, the committee prepares and forwards a letter to the other creditors informing them of the meeting that has just taken place with the debtor. The letter sets forth the financial information and requests that the creditors observe the moratorium and refrain from commencing or continuing any litigation.

2.22 Credit During Proceeding — The extension of credit during the workout period becomes the decision of the individual creditors, but most creditors will ship cash-in-advance or C.O.D. Suppliers are very cautious during this workout period because any obligations incurred by the debtor will be subject to discharge in a bankruptcy proceeding, and a supplier could very well find itself expanding upon the original debt which was subject to the moratorium.

2.23 Accountants — The accountants for the committee make an immediate cursory examination of the debtor s books and records to make sure that there have been no substantial preferences. It is imperative that the committee make a decision as to whether it wants to file an involuntary petition in bankruptcy, if there are such preferences, or whether creditors are better off in an out-of-court workout in spite of such preferences. In certain cases the creditors may also want to consider the impact of the difference in the treatment of reclamation claims in bankruptcy, but it would be unusual for this different treatment of itself to merit an involuntary.

2.23.1 — Once the fast, cursory examination is finished and the creditors have decided to keep the debtor out of bankruptcy, the accountants can take their time and look for any evidence of fraud, insider dealings, or the like. Again, assuming the existence of fraud or insider dealings, the committee must decide whether the case would be more properly administered in a bankruptcy proceeding.

2.24 Advantages and Disadvantages — There are advantages and disadvantages to the out-of-court workout. The disadvantages are that the committee has neither the power to set aside preferences nor the advantage of the so-called administrative powers that are provided for a trustee in a Chapter 11, such as the automatic stay, the rejection assumption or assignment of executory contracts or leases, or the protection that can be given to a secured lender when the debtor continues to borrow money. The debtor also does not have the right to defer the payment of taxes during a six-year period of time as it has in a Chapter 11, which can be meaningful in a case in which the debtor owes substantial taxes. Some of the advantages are that it is a more cost effective way to reorganize because there are no pleadings and memorandums or time consuming court hearings, and it is faster. The debtor also avoids supplier and customer relation problems that can flow from the filing of a bankruptcy proceeding, and the creditors probably realize a bigger return on their claims because of the percentage of acceptances needed for an effective composition. Of course, if the creditors conclude at any stage of the proceedings that bankruptcy is necessary, they may file an involuntary petition. The debtor may also file a voluntary petition in bankruptcy at any stage.

2.25 Involuntary — In those instances in which recalcitrant creditors file an involuntary during the course of a workout, the committee can join with the debtor and ask the bankruptcy court to abstain under Section 305 of the Bankruptcy Code. If the bankruptcy court makes the decision to abstain, the debtor and the committee will then be able to proceed to attempt to consummate the agreements arrived at during the course of the workout.

2.26 Plan Negotiation — If the debtor stabilizes its operations and is able to raise the necessary money to fund a workout, the debtor and committee follow a set process to negotiate a plan, which can be just as formal as in a Chapter 11 reorganization, depending on the case:

a.   The assets are appraised at a forced sale liquidation price.

b.   The debtor and the committee calculate the liquidation percentage to unsecured creditors, as that is the starting point in negotiations.

c.   The debtor attempts to negotiate peace with its secured creditors, as the agreement between the debtor and the committee cannot affect the rights of the secured creditor.

d.   The debtor and the committee then meet and negotiate an extension, a composition, or a combination of both. The creditors traditionally insist on a shorter deferred payout in an out-of-court workout than they would be willing to accept in a Chapter 11 proceeding.

2.27 Provisions in Plan — If the debtor and the creditors' committee are successful in negotiating a plan, an agreement is drawn up covering the understandings of the parties. This agreement has been referred to on different occasions as a moratorium agreement, composition agreement, forbearance agreement, extension agreement, or committee agreement. No matter what the documents are called, they typically contain provisions dealing with the following:

- A description of the settlement provisions
- Affirmative covenants
- Negative covenants
- Broad default provisions
- A procedure for the filing and resolving of claims
- A provision reinstating the original debt if the composed debts are not paid.
- A requirement for 90% acceptance, unless such requirement is waived by the debtor with the consent of the committee. The 90% acceptance requirement is not a formal requirement, but experienced practioners have found that an out-of-court workout is usually not effective unless accepted by approximately that percent of the debt.
- Execution of security agreements and mortgages to collateralize the payout.

2.28 Getting Acceptance — If an agreement has been reached and executed by the parties, a copy of this agreement, along with a letter from the committee to creditors extolling the virtues of the plan, a copy of the acceptance form, and perhaps a copy of the security documents, are sent to the general creditor body. The creditors are asked to complete the acceptance form and forward the form along with a proof of claim to a designated representative of the committee.

2.29 Binding Effect — The agreement becomes binding when the required percentage of acceptances is received. Once again, this agreement only binds those creditors who have accepted and agreed to participate. Those creditors who have not assented have a right to sue the debtor, but it is difficult for them to collect if the debtor has executed security interests and mortgages on its property as security for the benefit of accepting creditors. Because of this, the recalcitrant creditors usually agree to go along with the workout within a relatively short period of time.

3. LIQUIDATIONS

The principal methods for liquidating a business are:

(1) Liquidation under Chapter 7 of the Bankruptcy Code,

(2) Assignments for the benefit of creditors, and

(3) Corporate dissolutions.

The first two may be used by any type of business entity, whereas the third, as its name implies, only applies to corporations.

A. Liquidations under Chapter 7 of the Bankruptcy Code

Chapter 7 of the Bankruptcy Code contains the liquidation provisions and applies to individuals, partnerships, and corporations. There are, however, some provisions that apply differently to the different types of entities, such as discharge, exemptions, reaffirmation, and redemption. In addition, some provisions apply only to consumer bankrupts, but this article will not cover these areas. It is our intention to highlight only the liquidation of business bankrupts.

Chapters 1, 3, and 5 of the Bankruptcy Code are equally applicable to the liquidation and reorganization processes. Because many of these provisions were discussed above under Reorganization, we will make only a short reference to the sections in this portion of this chapter.

3.1 Eligibility — Any person who resides in the United States or has a domicile, place of business, or property in the United States may be a debtor under Chapter 7, except the following:

- A domestic insurance company, bank, savings bank, cooperative bank, savings and loan association, building and loan association, homestead association, or credit union.

- A foreign business of the nature described above engaged in such business in the United States.

A person is defined to include an individual, partnership, or corporation.

3.2 Filing — A liquidation case may be started in one of three ways: by conversion from Chapter 11 (either voluntarily or by court order), by the debtor's filing of a voluntary petition, or by the filing of an involuntary petition. If the debtor has 12 or more creditors, at least three creditors (whose claims total more than $5,000) must join in the involuntary petition. If there are less than 12 creditors, only one (whose claim is at least $5,000) is required. If the debtor is a partnership, a general partner or, if all of the general partners are in bankruptcy, the trustee of a general partner or any creditor of the partnership, may file the involuntary petition. An involuntary petition must allege and prove one of the two following grounds:

- General failure by the debtor to pay its debts as they become due, unless such debts are the subject of a bona fide dispute.
- The appointment of, or taking possession by, a custodian of substantially all the debtor's property within 120 days before the filing of the petition.

For the filing of a voluntary petition, there is no requirement that a debtor be insolvent.

3.3 Suspension or Dismissal — The court may dismiss or suspend a Chapter 7 case if the interests of creditors and the debtor would be better served by such dismissal or suspension. This order is not reviewable by appeal. This provision is frequently used when the debtor and creditors have been involved in an out-of-court workout and recalcitrant creditors file an involuntary petition. If the debtor and the general creditor body unite in their request for dismissal or suspension, it will frequently be granted by the Bankruptcy Court.

3.4 Duties of Debtor — The duties of the Chapter 7 debtor include:

(1) The responsibility to file a list of creditors, a schedule of assets and liabilities, and a statement of the debtor's financial affairs.

(2) Cooperating with the trustee to enable the trustee to perform his duties.

(3) Turning over all of the property of the estate and all books, documents, records, and papers to the trustee.

(4) If the debtor is an individual, appearing at the discharge hearing required under Section 524(d).

3.5 Trustee — Immediately after the entry of an order for relief under Chapter 7, the U.S. Trustee or the court, if there is no U.S. Trustee, must appoint a disinterested person to serve as interim trustee. This person is either a member of the panel of trustees or, if the debtor was in Chapter 11 and there was a trustee, that person. This interim service terminates when a permanent trustee is elected or one is designated, if no election takes place. The creditors have the right to elect a trustee at the so-called Section 341 meeting, if 20% of eligible creditors request such election. The interim trustee appointed by the U. S. Trustee must be disinterested and a member of the panel of private trustees.

3.5.1 — A person may serve as a trustee only if such person is:

- An individual who is competent to perform the duties of trustee, having an office in the judicial district within which the case is pending, or in any judicial district adjacent to such district.

- A corporation authorized by its charter or bylaws to act as trustee, having an office in at least one of the districts mentioned above.
- The U. S. Trustee for the judicial district in which the case is pending.

A person that has served as an examiner in a case may not serve as a trustee in the same case.

3.5.2 — The trustee is a representative of the estate and has the capacity to sue and be sued.

3.5.3 — The duties of the trustee include collecting and converting to cash all the assets of the estate, examining and objecting to claims, and filing the necessary accountings and reports. In the rare liquidation case in which the trustee is authorized to operate the business while it is being sold, the trustee must also file periodic reports of the operation with the Court, the U.S. Trustee, and taxing agencies.

3.5.4 — The trustee may hire attorneys, accountants, appraisers, and other professional persons that do not hold or represent an interest adverse to the estate and who are disinterested. The trustee is compensated in accordance with percentages set forth in the Code, whereas the professional persons are entitled to receive reasonable compensation for actual and necessary services rendered to the trustee.

3.6 Administrative Powers — The trustee in a liquidation case has the same Administrative Powers under Sections 361 through 366 of the Code as a trustee/debtor-in-possession has in a reorganization. (See §2.9 for a discussion of these powers.) In a liquidation case, the most important powers are the Automatic Stay under Section 362 and the power of sale under Section 363, although there are cases in which the trustee wishes to assume and assign a valuable executory contract or lease.

3.7 Property of Estate — The property of the estate in a liquidation case is the same as in a reorganization. (Refer to §2.10.) The trustee also has the same power to set aside preferences and fraudulent conveyances as in a reorganization. (See §2.11 for a discussion of these avoiding powers.)

3.8 Proofs of Claim — A creditor must file a proof of claim in a Chapter 7 case. This claim, according to Rule 3002, must be filed within 90 days after the first date set for the first meeting of creditors, except in certain instances the time for filing may be extended. In certain circumstances, the debtor or trustee may have the right to file a proof of claim on behalf of a creditor. No interest is allowed on unsecured claims after the date of the filing of the case. Note that the creditor must file a proof of claim even though the debtor scheduled the claim properly — the rule on filing proofs of claim in a Chapter 7 case is different from the rule (discussed at §2.12) in a Chapter 11 case. If the creditor actually filed a proof of claim in a Chapter 11 case, it need not refile if the case is converted to Chapter 7.

3.8.1 — See §2.12.2 for a discussion of which claims are entitled to priority;

the rules are the same in a liquidation.

3.8.2 — See §§2.12.3-2.12.5 for a discussion of the handling of claims of co-debtors, subordination, and undersecured claims.

3.9 Partnership Deficiency — If the debtor is a partnership and there are not enough assets to pay all claims, the trustee may collect the deficiency from the general partners of the debtor, first from those partners not in bankruptcy themselves, then from those in bankruptcy. There are also special rules for the treatment of tax claims and certain unsecured claims against a partner, when the partner and the partnership are in bankruptcy.

3.10 Priority of Distribution — The distribution of property of the estate to creditors, after it has been reduced to cash and after the secured claims have been paid or secured creditors have taken back their collateral, is in accordance with the priorities set forth in Section 726. The expenses of administration entitled to priority under Section 507 are paid first, then unsecured claims of creditors who filed proofs in a timely fashion or, if they filed tardily, did not have sufficient notice to file in a timely fashion. If there are assets remaining, other tardy claims are paid, then allowed claims for certain fines, penalties, and forfeitures. Excess assets go to pay interest on the above, with anything left going to the debtor.

3.11 Discharge — A debtor may receive a discharge of its debts in a Chapter 7 case, if the debtor is an individual. There are, however, reasons why a discharge of all of the debts may be denied and reasons why a discharge of specific debts may be denied (see 2.14 d). Reasons for denial of a general discharge include the debtor's violating the provisions of the Code or failing to fulfill its obligations thereunder and the debtor's failure to explain its loss of assets or inability to pay claims in full. A specific discharge may be denied of claims for certain taxes, or for fraud or misrepresentation claims, certain unscheduled claims, alimony claims, certain fines and penalties, and various other specified claims. As to certain of these nondischargeable claims, the creditor must file a timely adversary proceeding with the court seeking to have the debt declared not to be discharged. The others are automatically not discharged.

B. Assignment for Benefit of Creditors

3.12 Nature — To one extent or another the laws of all of the states allow a debtor to assign some or all of its assets for the benefit of creditors. Originally a common law device, this procedure has been codified by the laws of many states. The assignment may be a general assignment by the debtor of all of its property for the benefit of all of its creditors, a partial assignment in which a substantial portion of the debtor's property is not assigned, or a special assignment for the benefit of certain named creditors. The assignment is made by the debtor to an assignee, who holds the property or proceeds thereof in trust for the creditor-beneficiaries. The debtor, in making an assignment for benefit of creditors, retains no interest in the property, other than the right to receive back the excess proceeds, if any, after the creditor-beneficiaries are paid. Sometimes it is difficult to distinguish an assignment for benefit of creditors from a mortgage, the main test being whether the debtor has retained any control over the property or a right to redeem it. In fact, sometimes the assignment is in the form of a mortgage and/or security agreement with the trustee as the mortgagee/secured party. The trustee then forecloses and proceeds as though there had been a direct assignment.

3.13 Applicable Law — As mentioned, many states have statutes dealing with assignments for the benefit of creditors. Failure to comply with the statutes, however, may not prevent a valid common law assignment, depending on the particular state statute. Because the statutes vary, it is not possible to discuss the specific terms of each. Determining which state law applies is not always easy; it is usually the state in which the assignment is executed, but it may be the state in which the assignor resides or the assets are located.

3.14 Assignee's Duties — An assignment for benefit of creditors creates a trust relationship between the assignee and the creditor- beneficiaries. The applicable statute or common law will set forth the assignee's duties. These duties include liquidating the assets, notifying creditors, resolving disputed claims, and distributing the assets. To the extent the procedure is statutory, there will be court supervision.

3.15 Advantages and Disadvantages — There are certain advantages and disadvantages for creditors when .the debtor uses an assignment for benefit of creditors instead of liquidating under Chapter 7 of the Bankruptcy Code. The advantages are the relative speed and reduced expenses. The disadvantages include the following:

(a) creditors who do not consent are not bound by the provisions of the assignment, that is the claims of nonconsenting creditors are not discharged;

(b) the assignee does not have the avoiding powers that a trustee in bankruptcy would have; and

(c) the court does not have as broad jurisdiction.

Because creditors may be better served by a liquidation under Chapter 7, the debtor often calls a meeting of a few of its largest creditors, either before or just after the assignment is executed. At this meeting the debtor tries to convince the creditors that an assignment would be best. If the debtor fails, an involuntary bankruptcy is likely to follow. Before the creditors make a decision they usually retain attorneys and accountants to review the debtor's affairs to see if creditors will be hurt by the lack of avoiding powers.

C. Corporate Dissolutions

3.16 Methods — All of the state corporate statutes provide methods for dissolving corporations. These usually include:

(a) an automatic dissolution upon the expiration of the term for which the corporation was formed (although most states allow for perpetual existence);

(b) a voluntary dissolution approved by a majority (or possibly higher percentage) of the shareholders;

(c) a dissolution forced by one or more shareholders pursuant to an authorization in the articles of a corporation; and

(d) a dissolution ordered by a court for various reasons.

3.17 Suit to Dissolve — A lawsuit to dissolve a corporation can be filed by various people. For instance, the state attorney general may file a lawsuit to dissolve a corporation for reasons including repeated and willful exceeding of legal authority or repeated and willful conduct of business in unlawful manner. The shareholders or directors of a corporation may file a suit to dissolve it, if the directors are unable to agree on material matters respecting management of the corporation's affairs or the shareholders are so divided that they have failed to elect successors to the directors upon expiration of their term, and the corporation is unable to function effectively as a result. A minority shareholder may also sue to dissolve a corporation on the grounds that those in control are acting in a manner that is illegal, fraudulent or willfully unfair and oppressive to the corporation or the shareholder. The court in an action for dissolution has the power to dissolve the corporation or take such other, less drastic action sufficient to protect all the parties. The state attorney general (and possibly even creditors) may also be able to sue to dissolve a corporation on the grounds that it has been insolvent for a specified period of time.

3.18 Procedure After Dissolution — If a corporation is dissolved, with or without court action, it must give notice to its creditors, who then have specified times in which they must file claims. Procedures are then set forth for the handling of disputed claims and for a court to take over supervision of the liquidation in certain events.

3.19 Advantages and Disadvantages — For creditors of a corporation undergoing dissolution pursuant to state corporate statutes, there are advantages and disadvantages when compared with a liquidation under Chapter 7 of the Bankruptcy Code. The advantages are the reduced cost of the proceedings and the increased speed. The disadvantages are that the corporation does not have the avoiding powers available under the Bankruptcy Code, so the distribution to creditors may be less. Creditors may, therefore, file an involuntary bankruptcy petition, if they believe that the dissolution proceeding is not best for them.

4. TYPES OF SECURITY AND ENFORCEMENT

A. Land and Buildings

4.1 Evidence of Title — In most states, transfers of ownership are perfected by recording a deed with the Register of Deeds for the county in which the land is located. There is no document that evidences the title. Rather, the ownership of land can only be checked by examining the documents filed with the Register of Deeds. Usually this is done by checking a grantor-grantee index, tracking the title from one owner to the next. Sometimes, there is a tract index in which all of the transfers with respect to the individual tracts are noted.

4.2 Certificates of Title — In a few states interests in land other than leasehold interests are evidenced by a certificate, called a torrens certificate. Transfers of title are recorded on this certificate, which is evidence of the ownership in the land. Mortgages are similarly noted on the certificate.

4.3 Mortgages — Consensual liens on real property are, in most states, called mortgages. To be effective against subsequent holders of an interest in the real estate, the mortgage must be recorded with the Register of Deeds. Each state has specific requirements as to the form of the mortgage and execution thereof. Usually, the mortgage must contain a description of the property sufficient to identify it, and indicate the debt secured thereby. The mortgage must be signed by the mortgagor. In some states a mortgage cannot be recorded unless it is witnessed by two (sometimes three) witnesses. Notarization of the mortgagor's signature is almost always required for recording. An unrecorded mortgage is valid against the debtor but will not be valid against a subsequent transferee, except that in some states a subsequent transferee with notice of the unrecorded mortgage takes subject to it.

4.4 Foreclosure — If the mortgage contains a power of sale clause, most states allow the mortgagor to foreclose the mortgage upon default without filing a foreclosure lawsuit with the court. The specific requirements for a valid power of sale clause must be checked with each state, and the specific procedures for the actual foreclosure vary from state to state. If a power of sale clause is not valid in the particular state or was not contained in the mortgage, a suit to foreclose must be filed by the mortgagee upon default. The exact requirements for bringing this suit and the procedures must be checked in each instance.

4.5 Redemption — In most states, the mortgagor has a right to redeem from a foreclosure sale of real estate. The time for the redemption varies from one month to one year. To redeem, the mortgagor must pay the purchaser at the foreclosure sale the amount paid and any expenditures on the property made thereafter. In some states there is no right of redemption.

4.6 Deeds of Trust — In some states, documents known as 'deeds of trust' are used instead of mortgages. In such a document, the owner of the property deeds it in trust to a trustee for the benefit of the mortgagee. Other provisions regarding the enforceability and foreclosure of the deed of trust are basically similar to mortgages, but should be checked in each instance.

B. Personal Property (Tangible and Intangible)

4.7 Security Interest — In every state but Louisiana, security interests in personal property, whether tangible or intangible, are governed by a statute entitled the Uniform Commercial Code' ('UCC'). With minor variations, this statute is identical in each of the states. To be valid, a security interest must usually be evidenced by a writing. The only time a writing is not necessary is when the secured party has possession of the collateral pursuant to an agreement with the debtor. The writing may be titled security agreement,' 'chattel mortgage,' 'conditional sales contract,' or anything else. It need only evidence the intention of the debtor to grant the secured party a security interest in the collateral.

4.8 Debt Secured — Security interests can be granted to secure an old debt, debt being incurred at the time the security interest is granted, or a future debt.

4.9 Perfection — To be valid against most subsequent transferees of the collateral, including future secured creditors and lien creditors, notice of the security interest must be filed with the office or offices specified by the particular state s UCC. Many states provide only for filing with the Secretary of State. Other states provide for filing only with the local Register of Deeds. Some states provide for filing in both locations. In some the place of filing differs depending upon the type of collateral. The specific requirements of the individual state must be checked. The document to be filed may be the security agreement itself. Usually, however, a document entitled a 'financing statement' is filed instead. The financing statement contains the name and address of the debtor, the name and address of the secured party, and a description of the collateral. The financing statement must be signed by the debtor and, in a few states, the secured creditor.

4.10 Fixtures — A security interest may also be granted in tangible property becoming fixtures on real estate. To perfect such a security interest against subsequent owners of the property and subsequent mortgagees, a financing statement called a 'fixture financing statement' must be filed with the Register of Deeds where the property is located. In some instances the security interest in the fixtures may take precedence over an existing mortgage, and the UCC must be checked to determine when.

4.11 Foreclosure — Upon a default in the payment of the debt secured by a security interest, the secured party may foreclose. If the collateral is the accounts receivable of the debtor, the secured party forecloses simply by notifying the account debtors to pay the secured party. If the account debtors thereafter pay the debtor instead of the secured party, they may be liable to pay again. They may, however, require the secured party reasonably to prove the existence of its security interest. As to other collateral, the secured party must obtain possession, if it does not already have it. Usually this requires the secured party to file a lawsuit, often called a suit for claim and delivery. If the secured party can obtain peaceful possession of the collateral, a suit will not be necessary. If the debtor resists surrendering the collateral, court action is necessary. Taking the property from the debtor over its objections (even from a debtor clearly in default) without a lawsuit will expose the creditor to liability to the debtor. Because of this, peaceful repossession is usually only attempted with motor vehicles unless the debtor has consented to surrender the collateral.

4.12 Sale of the Collateral — Once the secured creditor has possession, it has several choices. First, it may attempt to keep the collateral in full satisfaction of the debt. To do so, it must give notice to the debtor and any junior secured creditor who has notified the secured party of its interest. The notice must say that the secured party intends to keep the collateral in full satisfaction of the debt. The people receiving the notice then have twenty-one days to object. If they do so, the secured party must sell the collateral. If the secured party does not wish to keep the collateral in full satisfaction, or if cannot do so, it must sell the collateral at a public or private sale. Reasonable notice of the time and place of a public sale or the day after which a private sale is to be held must be given to the debtor and any junior secured creditors who have notified the secured party of their interest.

4.13 Method of Sale — All provisions of a sale, whether public or private, must be commercially reasonable. That is, the secured creditor must do what is reasonable under the circumstances to obtain the highest price for the collateral, including advertising the sale and, in some instances, fixing the collateral. If the secured creditor has proceeded in a commercially reasonable manner, it will be able to pursue the debtor for any deficiency remaining after the collateral is sold, unless the security agreement has provided otherwise. A secured creditor who does not proceed in a commercially reasonable manner usually waives any deficiency. In some instances, it may even be liable to the debtor, if the debtor can show that the collateral should have brought more than the secured debt.

4.14 Motor Vehicles — If the collateral is motor vehicles covered by certificates of title, the secured party perfects the security interest by noting the security interest on the certificate of title. Filing of a financing statement is usually not required or sufficient. Perfection of a security interest in aircraft is made by filing with the Federal Aviation Administration.

4.15 Ships — If the collateral is a ship registered under the laws of the United States, instead of using a security agreement the secured party obtains a 'Preferred Ship Mortgage' from the debtor. This is then filed with the United States Coast Guard in Washington, D.C.

4.16 Patents and Trademarks — A security interest in patents and trademarks is perfected by filing with the Patent and Trademark Office in Washington, D.C.

C. Negative Pledges

4.17 Nature — Sometimes a creditor is willing to extend credit on an unsecured basis. To give itself some protection, however, it may obtain a negative pledge from the debtor. This is an agreement that the debtor will not give anyone a security interest or mortgage in the specified assets unless, at the same time, it gives the creditor an equal interest. If a future secured creditor has knowledge of the negative pledge, it will be bound thereby and required to share the collateral with the original creditor. Future secured creditors without notice of the negative pledge, however, will take free of it.

D. Guarantees

4.18 Enforceability — Guarantees are often required from the owners of a debtor or from affiliated companies. There is no question regarding the enforceability of a guarantee granted by the owner of the debtor, including its shareholders. There may be some problem, however, with a guarantee granted by an affiliated company, such as a subsidiary or sister corporation. Unless the affiliated company receives adequate consideration for the guarantee, creditors of the affiliate may seek to set it aside as a fraudulent conveyance if the affiliate becomes insolvent.

4.19 Security — Obviously, a creditor obtaining a guarantee obtains an even better guarantee if it is secured by assets of the guarantor. This security may be a mortgage on real estate and/or a security interest in personal property.

E. Debentures

4.20 Trust Indenture — If a company, partnership, joint venture, or corporation seeks to borrow money from numerous people, the debts are usually evidenced by debentures issued pursuant to a trust indenture. The trust indenture appoints a trustee, usually a bank, to enforce the debentures on behalf of the holders. Trust indentures are governed by the Federal Trust Indenture Act. If lending in a transaction governed by the act, the creditor should check the act, the provisions of the indenture, and the provisions of the specific debenture.

4.21 Security — Debentures issued pursuant to a trust indenture may be secured or unsecured. If secured, the provisions governing the security are the same as for any other debt. (See the discussion above regarding mortgages and security interests.)

5. DEBT COLLECTION PROCEDURES

A. Commercial Practice

5.1 Collection Before Suit — As in most countries, the collection of overdue accounts requires prompt attention and follow through. When written reminders and telephone calls do not obtain payment, there are collection agencies and attorneys that specialize in collection of commercial claims. Often requests by them for payment will be more productive because the debtor knows that legal action may be coming shortly.

5.2 Involuntary Bankruptcy — As mentioned earlier, three creditors whose claims total $5,000 may file an involuntary petition in bankruptcy. All they need prove is that the debtor is generally not paying its debts as they come due. Threat of such an involuntary is, of course, the ultimate collection measure, if the debtor believes the necessary elements are present and that the creditor will follow through with the threat. Short of filing an involuntary petition in bankruptcy, the creditor is left with legal proceedings to enforce its claim.

B. Legal Proceedings

5.3 State Procedures — Each state has its own procedures for collection of claims through lawsuits. Most states have different courts for claims of varying sizes, with one court hearing claims of approximately $10,000 or less and another court hearing larger claims. No creditor should seek to institute a suit against a debtor without legal counsel. The court's procedures are often strictly applied and, even in those limited situations in which a party may represent itself, legal counsel should be sought.

5.4 Costs — Although a prevailing creditor will get interest, at least from the date the complaint is filed, the costs awarded by courts are nominal at best. Usually the only costs awarded are the costs of the filing fee with the court and a very nominal attorney's fee. The cost of instituting an action must, therefore, be considered when the suit is for a small amount. Note that, if the debtor goes into bankruptcy, interest on unsecured claims will stop accruing from the date the petition is filed unless all claims are paid in full.

5.5 Obtaining Judgment — Once the suit is filed and the defendant is served with a copy of the complaint and a summons, the defendant will have a specified period within which to answer. If it fails to answer, the plaintiff will be entitled to take a default judgment. Many courts will enter a judgment based merely upon the facts alleged in the complaint. Other courts require more proof before the judgment will be entered. If the defendant answers the complaint, the parties will have a period of time in which to take discovery and then a trial will be held. If the plaintiff prevails at the trial, a judgment will be entered.

5.6 Enforcement of Judgment — Once the time to appeal from a judgment has passed, usually ten or twenty days, the plaintiff will be entitled to execute on the judgment. If the plaintiff knows where the defendant has assets, the plaintiff asks the court officer, usually a sheriff or the court bailiff, depending upon the court, to seize the property and sell it to pay the judgment. In the same manner, if the plaintiff knows where the defendant has a bank account, the plaintiff may garnish the bank account by having the court issue the necessary papers and then serving the bank. If the plaintiff does not know where the defendant has sufficient assets with which to pay the judgment, the plaintiff may take postjudgment discovery of the defendant regarding its assets. A writ of execution may also be recorded against real estate, giving the plaintiff a lien on the real estate. In some states, recording the judgment itself creates a lien on the real estate.

6. SOURCES OF LAW

A. Statutory Law

6.1 — Corporate law in the United States is governed by the statutes of each individual state. Similarly, each state will have its own laws governing partnerships and sole proprietorships. Public financing of companies is governed by federal legislation, the Securities Act of 1933 and the Securities Exchange Act of 1934 among others.

6.2 — Bankruptcies are governed by the Bankruptcy Reform Act of 1978, as amended. Each state may have its own laws governing assignments for benefit of creditors and corporate dissolutions.

B. Case Law

6.3 — All of the states of the United States, except Louisiana, are based upon the common law system in which cases play a great part. Major libraries in the various states, especially those in laws schools, will have the cases for all of the states. However, creditors should contact a lawyer in the particular state in question when a state law issue may be involved.

7. SOURCES OF INFORMATION

A. Federal Sources

7.1 — Companies that are registered with the Securities and Exchange Commission must file various periodic and special reports. Copies of these may be obtained from the SEC in Washington, D.C. Local brokerage houses may be able to furnish some of these reports.

B. State Sources

7.2 — Information regarding corporations is usually obtained from the Corporation Division of the Commerce Department of the individual state. Information regarding financing statements filed with the Secretary of State is usually obtained by writing the Secretary of State, Uniform Commercial Code Division. In addition, there are companies that will provide all of this information on a nationwide basis. Corporate information supplied by a corporation division will often be sparse, the name of the registered agent and the registered office sometimes being the only helpful information. Corporations are usually required to file annual reports listing the directors and giving a summary of the assets and liabilities. This information may also be helpful although dated. Although a copy of the articles of incorporation will always be on file, most are now forms and not very helpful.

C. Local Information

7.3 — Information regarding partnerships and sole proprietorships is usually obtained from a local office in which the business is conducted. Articles of partnership may be filed there as well as assumed name certificates.

D. Bankruptcy Information

7.4 — Information regarding bankruptcies must be obtained from the bankruptcy court in which the bankruptcy is pending. The court will provide copies of various papers filed with it. The fee is usually fifty cents per page. It is often best to consult an attorney when the case is pending to obtain the desired information. If a major bankruptcy is involved, there is sometimes a newsletter published that gives its subscribers periodic information regarding the progress of the case.

INDEX

Legend of country codes:
AUS = Australia; CAN = Canada;
UK = United Kingdom; US = United States